DONALD & MAUREEN GREEN

MUSIC CENTER

For the Love of Music

Donald & Maureen Green Music Center

Home of
Joan & Sanford I. Weill Hall
Schroeder Hall
Santa Rosa Symphony

Documentary Media

Seattle, Washington

For the Love of Music: Donald & Maureen Green Music Center
Home of Joan & Sanford I. Weill Hall, Schroeder Hall, Santa Rosa Symphony

Sonoma State University
1801 East Cotati Ave
Rohnert Park, CA 94928

First Edition
Printed in Canada

Primary Author: Jean Wasp
Project Manager: Susan Kashack
Project Executive Editor: Marne Olson
Designer: Paul Langland
Editor: Judy Gouldthorpe
Publisher: Petyr Beck

Produced by:
Documentary Media
books@docbooks.com
www.documentarymedia.com
877-935-9292

ISBN: 978-1-933245-39-3

Table of Contents

Dedications

An early view of the site of the Green Music Center. In the background is beautiful Sonoma Mountain to the east.

To Ruben Armiñana,

For the vision,

For the dream,

And the tenacity to overcome all odds.

To Donald and Maureen Green,

For the belief that dreams do come true and

For their love of music.

To Corrick and Norma Brown,

For their undying support and

For their love of community.

To Joan and Sandy Weill,

For their unflappable enthusiasm and

For helping to make dreams come true.

Marne Olson, Executive Editor

Foreword

The arts bring people together. Whether it is a Mahler symphony, a Jackson Pollock painting, a comedy by Molière or a sensitive poem by Dana Gioia, creative energy reaches out and pulls us in. A syncopating rhythm can lift us up from the difficulties of the day or a dramatic film can stimulate a discussion that brings about social change. Creative thought crosses boundaries and intellectual disciplines. What better place to have the Donald & Maureen Green Music Center, which celebrates music, the spoken word and the creative arts, than at Sonoma State University.

Over the past 17 or so years there have been stories, articles, interviews, records, and discussions of how the Green Music Center was first realized—how it came to be and what it took to get it open. It was time to get it down on paper. This history is done now, at least through the very special inaugural season of 2012 and the grand opening of Schroeder Hall in 2014.

The intense research and writing of the majority of this book was done by Jean Wasp, news & information coordinator at Sonoma State University. She somehow found the hours, weeks, days, months (and patience) to complete this task . . . and complete it well. My thanks to Jean for her excellent work and for those meetings we shared as we discussed issues, politics and what we wanted as a final product. Cheers to your care in writing these chapters and your in-depth research!

Equally important in the writing and production of this book is Susan Kashack, Sonoma State University's chief communications officer. I want to thank her for managing the project, as it was monumental in size and scope and had more than a few bumps, hopefully leaving us all with few bruises and many fond remembrances. Dealing with the hard questions that invariably come up when writing about so many different people and groups was a challenge, but together I feel we represented the story in truth, warts and all.

So many other people make a book come to life, and it did, indeed, take a village. Some of them are: Caroline Ammann, Doug Arias, Anne Biasi, Mike Conway, Juanda Daniel, Ryan Ernst, Nicolas Grizzle, Lori Hercs, Tyson Hill, Kelley Kaslar, Kindra Kautz, Jessica Markus, Casey Marshall, Linnea Mullins, Kamen Nikolov, Jennie Orvino, Sue Riley, Liam Robertson, Tai Russotti, Jeremy Vaughn and Ruth Wilson.

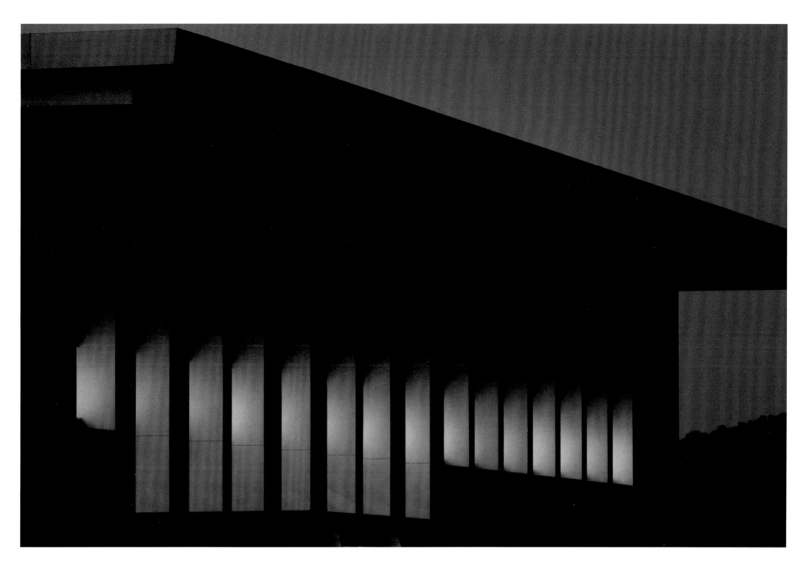

And lastly, I want to thank my husband, Ruben Armiñana, who is a visionary thinker who sometimes scares us all with his ideas. But I must say, with a few exceptions, he truly can see the future—and be ready for it when it arrives.

My sincere thanks to everyone who supported the Green Music Center project. You are very special people, and together we have made a very special place.

Sincerely,

Marne Olson

Vice-Chair, Green Music Center Board of Advisors

Executive Editor

A nighttime-lighted photo of the east side of Weill Hall.

Introduction

When Chinese piano sensation Lang Lang first graced the stage of Weill Hall at the Green Music Center in 2012, he stood in front of thousands of people—both inside and outside the hall—and said, "Let us now always try new things."

He was commenting on his performance of seven works that evening—three Mozart piano sonatas and four Chopin ballades—that he had never played before a live audience. But it also was a nod to the long and arduous journey that many had taken to make his appearance possible at a small university campus in northern California.

The journey has been full of high hopes, false starts, obstacles, critics, controversy, big promises and unexpected detours. The cast of characters surpassed what even Hollywood might have imagined. But it is also a story of how to renew one's vision and keep it alive in the most challenging of times.

Many hope the creation of the Green Music Center will lead to a re-emergence of the campus as a cultural arts destination for the region. The core mission has always been to "Aim high. Reach wide. Educate all."

It is a vision filled with great expectations. At the forefront are the ideas of the transformational power of the arts to educate and deepen one's connection to the world and how architecture can bring a community's cultural ambitions to life.

This rendering of the Green Music Center, including Weill and Schroeder Halls, gives an overview of the planned site, with tables on the terraced lawn and patrons on what became Weill Lawn.

A Performer's Dream

It was with great pleasure that I visited what later became Weill Hall at Sonoma State University less than a year before the hall opened in 2012. My friends Joan and Sandy Weill asked me to experience the hall and share my thoughts. They had heard of it, were impressed, and were considering becoming involved.

I arrived late one night after a performance in San Francisco's Davies Symphony Hall. I had not heard of the Green Music Center or even Sonoma State University. But I was more than pleased to visit and give my thoughts to my friends the Weills.

When I arrived, I saw a cluster of buildings that were close to completion; one or two appeared to already be open. The main hall, I could see, was framed between beautiful grounds and the magnificent hills behind it. Even though it was evening, the full moon illuminated the area.

As I entered the lobby of the hall, I was greeted by several members of the University staff. Inside the main hall I was met with a breathtaking space that reminded me of Ozawa Hall at Tanglewood, where I have enjoyed performing many times. In fact, the hall looked so similar I could have been in Massachusetts.

I sat down at the Steinway on the stage and began to play. Immediately I was taken by the manner in which the sound carried and how I was easily able to hear myself play. I have heard since that other performers have appreciated this as well.

It being nighttime, the hall was lit with warm golden light that highlighted the various and beautiful woods in the hall. I played for a while and knew that I would report to the Weills that they should certainly consider getting involved with the Green Music Center. They ultimately did, and the hall is now named for them: the Joan and Sanford I. Weill Hall.

I was invited to return for a performance on the inaugural weekend. Performing on that stage, with a full house of appreciative audience members, is an experience I wish to enjoy in future seasons.

The combination of a beautiful hall, a wonderful location in Wine Country, and warm summer evenings that allow for outdoor enjoyment, is a performer's dream. The fact that the acoustics truly are world-class only adds to the experience. I look forward to returning to Weill Hall again and again.

Lang Lang
Pianist

A Democratic Mission

Excerpted from the notes of Jeff Langley, founding artistic director of the Donald & Maureen Green Music Center, whose involvement with this project and its steering committee dates back to the Center's earliest days.

"From our first meeting, as we began to contemplate the possibilities, we were resolved that the mission and program of the Center would be an inclusive one—serving a broad segment of the campus and community and addressing broad tastes and perspectives in its programming. We'd been warned that multipurpose facilities, in trying to please everybody, often ended up satisfying no one, and we were ready for the challenge. Although our central goal was to design a flexible yet dedicated space ideal for acoustic music performance, we agreed that all forms of artistic expression, including dance and the spoken word, would be among the Center's core activities.

Jeff Langley

Taking our lead from Sonoma State President Ruben Armiñana, using Tanglewood, Aspen and some of the world's great arts festivals as a point of departure, we began to assemble and consider the elements that would make this center unique.

We started with location. Music and arts festivals are primarily summer events and draw from scenic, natural settings, which Sonoma County has in spades. Add wine to the mix, and it's easy to see a recipe for success. And yet, the Green Music Center would not only function in summer and not only include arts performances.

As a public university, our music, drama and dance students study the arts in the larger intellectual and social context of ideas. Our team of early planners became excited by the possibilities of joining and juxtaposing subject areas that seldom meet, much less interact: the principles of quantum mechanics anticipated in the violin sonatas of Johann Sebastian Bach, Dostoevsky meets Philip Roth, Alice in Wonderland meets Gertrude Stein, jazz improvisation as a metaphor for participatory democracy in America.

The Green Music Center would offer a total context for learning, where the line between student and teacher, performer and audience, participant and observer becomes, at times, indistinguishable. Driven by education and shaped by curriculum, the Green Music Center, we knew, had to be about learning, discovery, making connections—hands-on, up-close, participatory, innovative, reaching across disciplines and defying boundaries.

Perhaps most significant of all, we realized the Green Music Center could bring the University and the larger community together, creating a vital hub for cultural life in the entire North Bay region."

Professor and Chair of Music Brian Wilson conducts the Sonoma State University Brass Ensemble in the Trione Courtyard.

Tanglewood Tales

An artful rendering depicts Weill Hall ready for a performance, with the 54-foot rear folding panel doors open to the evening's warm Sonoma County weather.

Sonoma County is a paradise of endless sources of inspiration. It is the county of Jack London, Luther Burbank and the Bohemian Grove. With ancient redwood forests and oak-covered mountains, it also has 50 miles of stunning Pacific Coast views that delight visitors with wild, crashing waves beating against the shore, otters and sea lions sunning on the beaches, and spectacular sunsets that color the sky in brilliant hues. The county boasts visual artists, small theatre, wine appellations and much more. The ocean does much to ensure that the weather in the inland countryside is some of the most enviable in the world. These attributes, among others, draw visitors from south of the Golden Gate Bridge and from cities and states across the nation.

A rich agricultural area just 50 miles north of San Francisco, Sonoma County is also a major Wine Country playground, with premium wineries and farm-to-table dining. Grapes are the largest agricultural crop, and 60 percent are grown in multigenerational and family-owned vineyards. The world-class Sonoma wine region offers more than 400 wineries—from wine castles and the winery resort of Francis Ford Coppola, one of Hollywood's most famed directors, to simple and rustic tasting rooms.

Sonoma County also boasts more artists per capita than any other county in California. It has evolved into an artistic haven because of a mix of Bohemian and utopian ideals in its early history coupled with the very practical skills that come from the innovators who have settled here, said Tim Zahner, chief marketing officer for the Sonoma County Tourism Council. "People come here, whether to visit or settle, to be a part of the natural and contemplative world, and their art can spring from that."

The area is not unlike the rolling green landscape of the Berkshire Mountains in western Massachusetts, where Tanglewood and Ozawa Hall are located. There, as in Sonoma County, the interplay between art and nature leads to magical experiences.

Crossing the San Francisco Golden Gate Bridge to the north brings guests within an hour of the Green Music Center.

The 210-acre Tanglewood estate is the home of one of the nation's most acclaimed music education centers and an annual summer festival that is to classical music what Woodstock is to rock and roll. It has an enormous legacy in the realms of symphonic, chamber and vocal music, as well as opera and jazz, reaching the global music community. It has been called "the spiritual home of music in America."

Now in its 75th year, Tanglewood is the summer home of the Boston Symphony Orchestra. The illustrious lions of American classical music have studied there, grown their careers there, and brought their listeners to the edge of musical perfection there—from Aaron Copland, Leonard Bernstein and Seiji Ozawa to Michael Tilson Thomas, Stephanie Blythe, Wynton Marsalis, Zubin Mehta, Leontyne Price and others.

Hundreds of thousands of people make a pilgrimage to Tanglewood every summer to enjoy the concerts on a sprawling acreage where picnickers relax under New England skies. Located in the foothills of the Berkshire Mountains in Lenox, Massachusetts, the venue is named after a children's book of reimagined Greek fables by Nathaniel Hawthorne called *Tanglewood Tales*. Hawthorne came to the area in 1853 to write in a small cabin on the grounds of an estate, owned by a railroad baron, that was later named after the book's title.

In Sonoma County, different visions in need of a concert hall were germinating in the minds of three different groups of people in the mid-1990s. Two of them were looking for a new home for musical performances. One was hoping to reinvigorate a struggling regional university campus with a new future. They were all frustrated with the status quo.

Local vineyards are just one element of what makes Sonoma County an ideal location for an indoor/outdoor musical venue.

Tanglewood and its Seiji Ozawa Hall served as inspiration for bringing a similar-type hall to California and Wine Country.

Tanglewood Enchants

It was the very diversity of the scene at Tanglewood that always enthralled Marne Olson. Students carried their instruments across the lush lawn of the estate looking for a perfect spot to practice. Music filled the air from concerts featuring both classical and modern artists. The musical center in the Berkshires had been offering sublime experiences for decades, but when the new Ozawa Hall was completed in 1994, a new standard was achieved.

With a background in the arts and politics, Marne Olson had been to Tanglewood many times before, taking seminars in orchestra management, attending workshops and enjoying concerts—and she had attended the last concert conducted by Leonard Bernstein. Her husband, Dr. Ruben Armiñana, was named president of Sonoma State University in 1992, and he joined her one year at Tanglewood.

Four years into his administration, Armiñana was eager to resuscitate what was primarily a college commuter campus. When he had first taken the post, he found that the school was floundering financially. He was charged with reinventing SSU. It was his first university presidency, and he would spend most of his administration transforming it to better meet community and student needs.

While in Tanglewood in 1997 at a nearby arts and higher education conference, Armiñana and Olson saw the newly constructed Seiji Ozawa Hall for the first time. They were impressed with how it delivered on its promise of acoustical excellence.

A world-class concert hall had been built with an innovative sliding back barn door, not common for venues of its type. It opened the concert hall to thousands of picnickers on the lawn outside. This allowed for a vibrant summer season, not hard to imagine being done California-style in the Wine Country. Armiñana is fond of telling the story that he said, "I want one" for the SSU campus because "our weather is better" and "we have no flying insects."

President Ruben Armiñana and his wife, Marne Olson, came to Sonoma State University in 1992. By then, Marne had already attended many masterful performances at Tanglewood.

Silicon Vineyards

Donald Green, a talented engineer who, for decades, was a gifted entrepreneur, became known as father of the area's legendary Telecom Valley. He and the engineers he mentored founded many of the companies thriving there. Many became newly minted millionaires, thanks to a telecommunications industry boom. The area became so wealthy that it was sometimes called "Silicon Vineyards."

Donald Green in his early days as an engineer and budding entrepreneur.

Green was savvy enough to know that his companies could more easily draw sophisticated and talented employees to the area if it had cultural benefits. He and his wife, Maureen, loved the challenge and complexities of singing Bach choral works and had sung in choirs everywhere they lived for decades. They helped found Sonoma State University's Bach Choir. But there was no acoustically appropriate space on campus for the choir to perform or rehearse, so they moved from venue to venue (usually local churches) each season. Most locations were limited in size, with myriad acoustical challenges. When they'd finally had enough shuffling around, the Greens decided they would fund the building of a choral space on the Sonoma State University campus with a $1 million gift.

SSU Choral Director Bob Worth was more than stunned when Green first proposed the concept over lunch one day in 1996. The idea hinged on one of his companies having a successful public launch, which it soon did.

Donald and Maureen Green first connected to Sonoma State University through their singing in the University's Bach Choir.

It did not take much time before the Greens' idea for a choral space merged with Armiñana and Olson's idea of a Tanglewood-like venue at Sonoma State University. At a dinner to explore mutual visions for a music facility at SSU, the Greens gained an expanded view of the possibilities, which led to increasing their original gift to $5 million.

There was just one character left to enter the stage—a resident orchestra.

A Leap of Faith

The Santa Rosa Symphony, one of the oldest symphony orchestras in the western United States, was ready to take a leap to the next level. Frustrated with the acoustical limitations of what was then the Luther Burbank Center for the Arts in Santa Rosa, a former church where patrons still sat on wooden pews, the musicians knew that a new venue would enable the orchestra to fulfill its destiny. The solution was possibly 10 minutes away, in Rohnert Park. How they would convince their subscriber base to drive several miles from Santa Rosa to a new location on the SSU campus was one of their biggest concerns.

Corrick Brown was the Santa Rosa Symphony's second music director, serving from 1957 to 1995.

After relentless discussions, a deal was struck that gave the Santa Rosa Symphony a 25-year lease as the resident orchestra. In return, they committed to raise funds for the project.

Corrick Brown, the conductor emeritus of the Santa Rosa Symphony, thought that funding a first-class concert hall was within reach and was something few communities across the country could ever imagine, let alone actualize. "This is a turning point in the history of the arts in Sonoma County," he said. "We are building the crown jewel for the region."

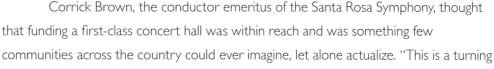

Jeffrey Kahane was the Santa Rosa Symphony's third music director, from 1995 to 2006.

Santa Rosa Symphony music director Jeffrey Kahane knew well where he was leading his orchestra. "Only when the audience finally hears the orchestra in a hall designed specifically for music will they appreciate a new horizon of listening," he said. "When that music meets the audience, the transformation will be breathtaking."

With the trinity of visionaries in place, the Center for Musical Arts, as it was first called, was born. Since it would be on a university campus, the vision quickly expanded to include a 1,400-seat main concert hall, a 250-seat recital hall, practice rooms, faculty offices, lobby/hospitality space and recording facilities. The budget was set at $22 million, based on preliminary estimates of construction and design costs and probable donor commitments.

For several months one year, fanciful wooden cutouts graced the berm on the east side of the Green Music Center site, artist unknown. The pieces disappeared as quietly as they first appeared.

The Santa Rosa Symphony had already established a reputation as having one of the most comprehensive music education programs for young people in the nation, with five youth ensembles and a music academy. The Symphony would complement the University's music programs.

Jeff Langley, artistic director of the Center for Musical Arts and the Center for Performing Arts at SSU, said, "This will be the crowning glory for the region. With the merits of the University and a great symphony orchestra, the cultural landscape of our community will be enhanced for generations to come."

— Jean Wasp

Tanglewood Trip Advising

My job was to make arrangements for trips of donors and members of the University to visit Tanglewood and experience its beauty and elegance. The first time I organized a trip was in 1998. There was a lot of intense work involved in arranging the trips—travel arrangements, accommodations, performance tickets, lunches, dinners, blankets, ice chests . . . the list seemed endless. But it was worth it to share the magic of Tanglewood and Seiji Ozawa Hall with our people. Music wasn't just something to listen to sitting in Ozawa Hall; it was something to be experienced, and something to surround yourself with, as the musicians and the building itself worked together to transport the sound from the performers to your ears. Music experienced sitting outside Ozawa Hall beneath the stars was different but equally magical. These experiences were invaluable to the understanding of the importance of our project at Sonoma State University. I am pleased and honored that I was able to play a small part in making the dream of the Green Music Center a reality.

Anne Handley
Tanglewood Traffic Coordinator

The Green Music Center has been a good part of my life for the last 15 years, thanks to Don and Maureen Green, Ruben Armiñana and Marne Olson, and more recently Joan and Sandy Weill.

Since the Santa Rosa Symphony was to be the resident orchestra of the new hall, I signed on as one of the three "accents" to raise funds, joining the English Green and the Cuban Armiñana. I was the California Brown! We gave talks at what might have been hundreds of receptions, large and small, for the next 12 years or so. Our message: "This is going to be great and you want to know about it."

In the end, I was invited, after 55 years of conducting, to direct the national anthem followed by Beethoven's overture The Consecration of the House *at the opening of Weill Hall in September 2012. Were all those years of fundraising worth it? Indeed, and then some. The sound is as beautiful as the hall. Coming to play in this wonderful hall along with our own orchestra was a particular joy for me and the several thousand ticket holders who have*

enjoyed and supported the Santa Rosa Symphony for its 85+ years. Even the world-famous Vienna Philharmonic played in Weill. And they loved the hall!

Corrick and Norma Brown
Conductor Emeritus
Santa Rosa Symphony

I first met Don and Maureen Green at the home of Bob Worth, SSU's choral director, in the late 1980s. The Greens were members of the Bach Choir, and the choir was planning a trip to Mexico. I was at the meeting with the group to explain how they could raise money to support the trip since many members of the choir were students and would need financial assistance.

In 1996, Don had taken Bob Worth to lunch, and as he was returning him to the campus, he mentioned that if things went well with Advanced Fibre Communications, Don would gift a million dollars to build a facility on the campus that the choir could perform in.

The following year, Ruben and Marne had gone to Tanglewood and seen Ozawa Hall. At a cabinet meeting, Ruben suggested this kind of facility would be much better located in Sonoma County because it could be used all year round.

Soon after, Don and Maureen and Shirley and I were invited to dinner at the Armiñanas. At that time, Ruben described the facility at Tanglewood. By the time dinner was over, Don and Maureen Green had committed $5 million to the project after just viewing a single brochure. They agreed to visit Tanglewood as well. Two weeks after returning from our Tanglewood trip, Maureen and I met for lunch at Equus, and at that time she committed an additional $5 million matching gift. If we raised the same amount of money, they would match it. Thanks to a very generous community, we were able to do so.

Jim Meyer
Vice President for Development
1980-2001

2 | A Do-able Insanity

*I*n Ruben Armiñana's sixth-year presidential evaluation in 1998, California State University Chancellor Charles Reed noted a faculty member's comment, "The area in which he is most criticized is when he brings forth ideas . . . this is what frightens people."

The SSU president has often called the Center for Musical Arts project "a do-able insanity." "My vice presidents thought I was crazy when I first proposed it," Armiñana recalled. But he moved quickly to make it happen.

Seizing upon a brochure at Tanglewood about the creation of Ozawa Hall, he called design architect Bill Rawn and talked with him about creating a similar hall at Sonoma State University. "The call came from out of the blue," said Rawn. "Often, these kinds of things never amount to anything more than a fishing expedition. But Ruben had a clear idea of what he wanted. He was very articulate about what he wanted for Sonoma State, articulate about Ozawa Hall, which had caught his imagination. It was obvious he had given it a lot of thought. To this day I'm amazed at the clarity of his vision to go ahead and do it."

In a time of continual state budget crises, Armiñana often pulled out that Tanglewood brochure to perpetuate the "do-ability" of a music center on the SSU campus. It was all to be accomplished through private donations.

Unbeknownst to the SSU president, Rawn, whose architectural firm was in Boston, was a native Californian. Born in Berkeley, he grew up in Southern California. Every summer he visited an aunt and uncle in Napa County. He had recently started work on the Carneros Inn project in Napa. This gave Rawn a California sensibility that would inform his sense of the land, an important principle that is reflected in all of his work. "The Napa-Sonoma landscape is deep in my soul," he said.

The rear wall of Weill Hall opens to seat an additional 5,000 guests on the terraced Weill Lawn and adjacent grassy areas.

Ozawa Hall at Tanglewood was the first concert hall that Rawn and his firm had ever built. The concept of the sliding barn door at the back of the hall was a pioneering idea. That is what primarily intrigued the SSU president and his wife, Marne Olson, who wanted a year-round facility for the campus.

Rawn had immediately turned to acoustician Larry Kirkegaard for help in building Ozawa Hall, and later he would do the same for the SSU music project. Guided by Kirkegaard, who knew the territory well, Rawn and his associates spent months investigating the attributes of the finest concert halls in the world in their preparation for building Ozawa.

The granddaddy of all concert halls is Vienna's Musikverein, said to produce the "Golden Sound in the Golden Hall." It was built in the mid-1800s, when no science of architectural acoustics existed. Constructed in a "shoe-box" style, the design drives sound around in a way that provides for a superb listening experience. Rawn and Kirkegaard's version, Ozawa Hall, did not disappoint.

Search for the Perfect Site

Bill Rawn visited SSU in 1998 to meet with Armiñana and Olson, who showed him possible sites on campus as well as the local countryside. "We were soaking up Sonoma from their point of view and not from our own memories," said Rawn.

 Rawn then took off on his own to walk the campus and found himself along a waterway called Copeland Creek, on the north edge of the campus. A small trail led to a flat field with hills to the east and northeast that formed a bowl at the intersection of Rohnert Park Expressway and Petaluma Hill Road.

"We immediately started imagining the audience facing north and east, understanding that they would be looking at an angle at the sheep-herding hills and that they could see the hills without being distracted," said Rawn. "We at least owed it to Ruben to mention this field, though we knew that SSU did not own it."

Armiñana was unfazed. He said, "We are very ingenious at Sonoma State, and the University has to grow." He agreed that the location was spectacular. Rawn expected the land purchase alone to take a long time. But the University had the purchase from several property owners, including Tom and Kay Reed, rolling within months. It would enlarge the campus by 43 acres.

While fundraising and other tasks were under way, so were the seemingly endless decisions about design, materials, and the look and feel of the Center. The design and other elements of what later became the Green Music Center and Weill Hall came not only from Rawn, but also from an ongoing group of key players such as Don and Maureen Green, artistic director Jeff Langley, executive director Floyd Ross, Ruben Armiñana, Marne Olson, Larry Furukawa-Schlereth, Bruce Walker, Christopher Dinno and others.

"We wanted to be sure that this was being designed as a California facility—not a Tanglewood, a Benaroya or a Ravinia. They are all beautiful, but a California performance space would be quite different in feel from any of the other great halls of the world," said Marne Olson, now vice-chair of the Green Music Center Board of Advisors.

In their local travels, Armiñana and Olson would see beautiful uses of color, space or texture elements that they would bring back to the architects to incorporate into the design. Sometimes a color scheme at a restaurant would seem the perfect element for the Center, or a stone wall they saw at a building in Sacramento, with a warm, inviting feel. The wisteria-draped pergola that is situated on the great lawns of Tanglewood or the colors of a museum courtyard would catch their eye as something that would fit well in California. Of particular interest to them was Landmark Vineyards in Kenwood, with its rustic and serene grounds and mountains that serve as a backdrop to the fields of grapevines. In fact, they took Rawn to the vineyard to capture the "feel" of the elements and colors.

In designing the Center they also knew there should be a lobby and other spaces for events and fundraising, including outdoor courtyards and a dining venue. "Those are all areas Ruben and I wanted to be sure we incorporated in the Center," said Olson. "When you include all of those areas, it is going to cost more—but it would bring more flexibility to do whatever is needed in the future."

Some aspects of the Green Music Center have changed since its inception, but the indoor/outdoor capabilities of the hall remain as seen in this early architectural rendering.

Fundraising Takes Flight

One afternoon, Armiñana brought out the Tanglewood brochure at the Sebastopol home of Jim Meyer, the University's vice president for development. Meyer thought they were meeting about how to cover a million-dollar campus deficit. Instead, he found himself looking at a pamphlet about Seiji Ozawa Hall and a new mission for the University.

Fundraising efforts began in earnest with trips to Tanglewood for potential donors and staff to deepen the understanding of the project. Don and Maureen Green were the first to go, during Tanglewood's summer festival in 1997, and saw the impact on the community—performances, students training with master musicians, rehearsals, and a general feeling of inspiration. They too were captivated by the magic of Tanglewood and returned home to double their gift to $10 million. Armiñana took his staff that same year—Jim Meyer, Jeff Langley (chair of SSU's Center for Performing Arts), and John Bond (facilities director)—to begin to develop SSU's effort.

Meanwhile, thanks to the Greens' generosity, the CSU Board of Trustees voted in May 2000 to name the facility, in perpetuity, the Donald & Maureen Green Music Center.

Ozawa Hall had been built for $10 million. But Armiñana figured the University could easily handle the higher construction costs—due mainly to California's seismic, environmental and accessibility standards and the fact that SSU's center would be year-round as opposed to summers only at Ozawa—because so much had already been donated.

In 2000, Sonoma State University established the Green Music Festival, a summer concert series intended to help spread the word about the Green Music Center and ramp up support for the capital campaign. An inaugural festival featured two outdoor concerts by the Santa Rosa Symphony—an Independence Day pops concert and a Midsummer Night on the Green. It attracted thousands of patrons that first year and continued to grow audiences over the nine years it was held.

With Ozawa Hall at Tanglewood as a cost indicator, it was estimated that the main hall of the Green Music Center would be a $10 million project.

Professor Bob Worth leads the SSU Chamber Singers at the ground-breaking ceremony in October 2000.

Soon afterward, the University launched Greenfarm, working with the Santa Rosa Symphony, its board president Creighton White, and its youth programs. A summer music and performing arts academy, Greenfarm offered hands-on, interactive learning for hundreds of children from ages 5 to 18 as well as courses for professionals.

On a rainy but hopeful day in October 2000, the University held a ground-breaking ceremony. The event's program showed the new dimensions of the project: $43 million budget; $25 million committed; $18 million to complete the capital campaign. The project had expanded during the design phase but the main concepts remained— a concert hall on one end, a recital hall on the other, and integral to it all, an exciting new home for music education, later named Music Education Hall by then-Provost Eduardo Ochoa.

The day was overcast and a persistent breeze kicked up whirlpools of dust from the field. Power was supplied to the site by a modified BMW that one of the theatre arts techs had transformed into an electric car. Choral Director Bob Worth led a short performance by the SSU Chamber Singers. Doug Morton, lead trumpet with the Santa Rosa Symphony, presented a fanfare called *Intrada* for the Green Music Center.

At some point, it started to rain. The downpour let up just as Donald Green began to speak about the future promise of the Center. University officials and major donors used ceremonial shovels to lift dirt into a mound in a gesture of optimism for the future.

Everything seemed possible that day. Little did that pioneering band of entrepreneurs, local arts patrons and University officials know that a perfect storm was headed their way.

Left to right: Marne Olson, Larry Gould, Jeffrey Kahane, Maureen Green, Don Green, Corrick Brown and Ruben Armiñana put the first shovels to the earth at a groundbreaking ceremony in 2000.

Green Music Festival –
In All Ways, a Celebration of
Music, Arts and Ideas

For nine years, the Green Music Festival was a summer production on the SSU campus. Always an eclectic array of music that filled the months of July and August, it was the first example—in real time—of what the founders of the project envisioned.

"It was an opportunity to show people what this European-style concert hall project was all about, what the programming would mean for the future, and what the overall experience could become," said Alan Kleinschmidt, Festival marketing director. "We had to do well, without a hiccup, because we were promoting a vision of a world-class concert hall, and it had to have the feel of a high-end event or we would not have succeeded in these early stages, let alone attract new donors."

Organizers aimed high and reached wide from the very beginning. The legacy of Tom Birdsall, the Greens' son-in-law, will always be about his leadership in launching a successful Festival working alongside Jeff Langley, artistic director of the GMC, and Floyd Ross, GMC executive director. Together they shaped what the Festival would become. And that vision stayed strong and clear throughout its run.

Ravinia's renowned summer festival near Chicago and Tanglewood's music education and concert festival in Massachusetts were in their sights as models, but with a West Coast twist. The goal was simple but ambitious: to become one of the major cultural arts festivals in the United States. Begun the same year as the first groundbreaking for the Green Music Center, the festival season was created in order to ramp up enthusiasm for and awareness of what was to come.

Media partners joined early on to support the effort and provided substantial publicity that was crucial to the Festival's early and continued success. The local daily, *The Press Democrat*, published a special print supplement each year to describe the Festival's vision, virtues and programs to its readers.

KDFC radio, the San Francisco classical music station, sent its popular host Hoyt Smith to interview Jeffrey Kahane on the Festival grounds for several seasons. This spread the word about the new festival, as well as the Green Music Center project, to Bay Area classical music fans.

Tom Birdsall launched the successful Green Music Festival to raise funds and build enthusiasm for and awareness of the Green Music Center project.

KJZY, the local jazz station, pumped up enthusiasm for the jazz element in the Festival programming and laid the groundwork for appearances by many well-known jazz artists.

The unsung heroes of the Festival were the extraordinary University staff from across the entire campus. SSU employees and community volunteers worked double duty to bring the Festival performances to life. After working a full week, many staff would be back early on the weekend and work through the evenings to make sure the performance sites were ready for the artists and patrons. "The Festival simply would not have been possible without their dedication and professionalism," said Kleinschmidt.

Lacking a building to illustrate the vision, Festival staff used a cardboard model of the proposed Center, developed by architects, to educate the public about the unfamiliar shoe-box shape. It was a big challenge to inform and inspire the public about what was promised to be "a gathering place for all," said Kleinschmidt. "People got behind the idea and began to embrace it as their own."

One Summer at a Time

The Festival season was built one summer at a time, beginning in 2000. The first festival was called the Festival on the Green and set the tone for those that followed.

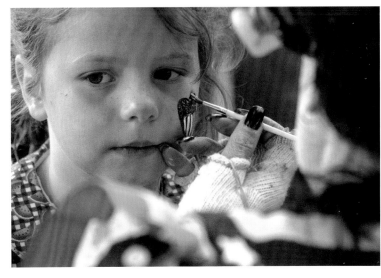

The inaugural Festival on the Green in 2000 inspired a lively atmosphere and a day of old-fashioned Americana, with picnics, music and fireworks to celebrate Independence Day.

Nearly 5,000 attended the first July 4th celebration—Independence Day on the Green—and heard big band music from the '40s, Gershwin tunes and patriotic standards performed by the Santa Rosa Symphony.

People brought their food baskets and folding chairs, and dressed in Old Glory. Some had decorated their desserts in red, white and blue. It was old-fashioned Americana and it was great fun on the campus lawn.

Historical figures dressed as John Adams, Eleanor Roosevelt, Amelia Earhart, Thomas Jefferson and Thomas Paine gave speeches to anyone who would listen. A special play area offered games, jugglers, crafts, face painting, storytelling and food for the younger attendees. Dazzling fireworks ended the evening, launching a new family-style tradition on the campus.

Performing arts staff and students got into character to help celebrate the inaugural Festival on the Green in 2000.

The other event that first year was a romantic evening in August called Midsummer Night on the Green. Conducting the Santa Rosa Symphony, Jeffrey Kahane presented a Mendelssohn, Rachmaninoff and Tchaikovsky program.

In 2001, Kahane was eager to reach for the stars when he was named the Festival's artistic director. Attendance that second year nearly doubled, to 8,500. As part of the July 4th program, he presented Gershwin's *Concerto in F* before the fireworks filled the evening skies. The 2001 Midsummer Night on the Green was an all-Tchaikovsky program.

That same year, Latin music gained a foothold at the Festival when Cuban-themed Jazz on the Green made its first appearance with Grammy winner Joe Lovano and his eight-piece ensemble. Jazz artists who performed over the years included Cuban jazz composer-pianist Gonzalo Rubalcaba, singer-songwriter Albita, and Poncho Sanchez. Trombonist Jimmy Bosch and his band and violinist Lelia Josefowicz presented a dueling rendition of Vivaldi's *Four Seasons*.

"Albita hit one out of the park," said Kleinschmidt. Salsa lessons for 2,000 people had primed the audience for a real Latin experience.

The first Jack London lecture series, in 2001, was the seed for later programs exploring the famous author's world and his relationship to the various California land-scapes in his writings. Free fireside tales for families relaxing under the stars were read by local celebrities who chose their favorite London stories to share. The finale was the production in 2006 of the Sonoma City Opera's *Every Man Jack*, a newly commissioned opera based on London's groundbreaking autobiographical work *John Barleycorn*.

Top: In 2001, Latin jazz was added to Festival on the Green, with delightful stage performances by Grammy winner Joe Lovano and others.

Bottom: A salsa lesson gets the crowd in the mood for dancing at the second annual Festival on the Green, in 2001.

In 2002, the third season, the name was changed to the Green Music Festival. The first chamber music series was added to the program offerings. "Jeffrey Kahane and Friends" was an instant success. It was so popular that in 2003, Kahane doubled the number of his "musical friends" invited from major American orchestras as well as solo artists with international reputations.

> *Music . . . can name the unnameable and communicate the unknowable.*
>
> — Leonard Bernstein

The third season also brought an Ansel Adams Centennial exhibition to the Sonoma State University Art Gallery, thanks to the connections and work of the Greens' son-in-law Tom Birdsall. It featured 70 original prints with an emphasis on images of Northern California and Sonoma County, celebrating the great photographer's centennial birthday.

As the years rolled on, world-class musicians continued to perform on the Festival stage in the 475-seat Evert B. Person Theatre. New programs were introduced: dance by the Sean Curran Dance Company, a special benefit performance by Carol Channing for performing arts students, and a conversation with Willie Brown, California State Assembly Speaker emeritus.

The Pacific Mozart Ensemble, directed by SSU music professor Lynne Morrow, staged a multimedia presentation called *A Story of Freedom,* an evening of spirituals that mirrored the history of African-Americans in the United States. The piece was written by Morrow, who calls spirituals "the original chamber music."

In 2007, Independence Day on the Green was put on hold. Fireworks would not again fill the skies over the campus until 2012 at the inaugural weekend opening of Weill Hall.

Organizers decided to make 2008 the final year for the annual Green Music Festival, in order to focus on the fundraising campaign to complete the Green Music Center project. The last season showcased performers from the local region, offering vocal and instrumental jazz artists, choral ensembles, high-energy gypsy music and dance, and cutting-edge chamber music.

Overall Festival attendance reached 30,000 at its peak. The value of those first nine years of music, arts and ideas became apparent in 2012 when the Green Music Center performance seasons in Weill Hall began under the sponsorship of MasterCard.

— Jean Wasp

Greenfarm – Discovery Through the Arts

In June and July for six summers, Ives Hall on the Sonoma State campus resonated with the sounds of young voices in song, while classically trained performers on all instruments passed on their love of music to talented young players ranging from beginners to advanced-level performers. Across the way in Person Theatre, apprentice teen actors discovered the secrets of the stage through comprehensive classes in acting, singing and dancing.

These activities and more were part of Greenfarm, the arts and education component of the Green Music Center. Greenfarm embodied the Green Music Center's commitment to establishing the arts and arts education as a vital, thriving and indispensable part of the community.

Running from 2001 to 2006, Greenfarm was the first step in creating a legacy of music and arts education that would resurface in a new form with the Weill Hall Artists-in-Residence program and expanded K-12 partnerships in the area after the Center opened in 2012.

Partnering with the Santa Rosa Symphony's Summer Music Academy and Sonoma State University faculty, Greenfarm harnessed conservatory-level training opportunities from professional Bay Area musicians, actors and dancers. It provided a space to bring it all together with performances of symphonic, chamber and choral music, dance, and original theater pieces during the summer.

Offering academic-enrichment classes for youths and music-education training for teachers, the program grew to include pre-professional and professional divisions with advanced studies in opera, chamber music and voice.

Performances took place throughout the five-week program, culminating in Greenfarmfest, a final youth festival weekend in late July, featuring two days of performances, guest artists and a celebration barbecue for participants and their families.

— Ruth Wilson
SSU Music Department Publicist

Each summer from 2001 to 2006, Greenfarm brought K-12 students to SSU for music and performing arts education, culminating in the Greenfarmfest festival in July.

Youths at Greenfarm received conservatory-level music training from masters such as Jeffrey Kahane.

Unsung Heroes

I was always so impressed with the unsung heroes of the early Festival seasons: John Connole, working on a 100-degree summer day to get lights up for a Fourth of July display; Mary Rogers and Shelley Martin putting small flags on the picnic tables on the lawn to create a patriotic spirit; Michael Bearden, Ron Bartholomew, Jenny Juhl, Liam Robertson, Russ Wigglesworth, Kamen Nikolov, and many more working long days and nights on the weekends to make sure the patrons had an experience they would remember. Everyone really stepped up and represented the University at a very high level. And then it was back to work on Monday to their "day" jobs.

Alan Kleinschmidt

Marketing Director
Green Music Festival
Center for Performing Arts
Sonoma State University

Doing Our Homework

Any institution, be it educational or civic, is well advised to do extensive homework prior to architects putting pencil to paper. There is enormous value in having a point-person involved from day one representing the end users of the facility. For the Green Music Center project, I was that representative. As one of a small number of key members of the University community who were involved from the very beginning, I was fortunate to be able to experience firsthand performances in some of the finest concert halls, performing arts centers, summer festival venues and music education facilities in the U.S. and Europe. We asked questions of both administrators and stage personnel in order to gain a broad understanding of what we hoped to achieve.

Our project was made easier because Ruben Armiñana provided the team with a clearly articulated vision and by engaging the same design team responsible for Tanglewood's Ozawa Hall. Over the course of several years, our concert hall project grew to include education, hospitality, recital and outdoor venues.

With our homework done, with close attention paid to details, and with a single-minded focus on the vision, this extraordinary world-class venue designed for education and performance is our legacy to be enjoyed by future generations of students, artists and patrons.

Floyd Ross
Executive Director, Green Music Center
2000-2009

People often ask me about my job and what it entails. I oversee the production operations at the Green Music Center. The vast majority of my work is technical, such as stage setup, loading and unloading gear, sound and lights, audio and video recordings, rigging, and anything else that the artist needs to get ready for her/his performance.

I still remember the first ribbon-cutting and groundbreaking ceremony in the early 2000s. One of the memories I will have with me forever was trying to figure out a way to have electrical power and a sizable sound system for the groundbreaking, which was to be held in the middle of an open field. The performers were the local Children's Choir. We didn't want to bring in a generator, because it was going to be too noisy and overpower the gentle voices of the little children singing. The solution finally emerged. One of the employees of the theatre arts department, Michael Bearden, had built a fully electric vehicle years before any existed. I was shocked when he rewired things and soon we had regular household electrical power. We used it to amplify the sound and everything went perfectly smoothly.

Kamen Nikolov

Director, Production Operations

Green Music Center

What moves you? Opportunity. The endless amount of opportunity that Sonoma State University has embodied throughout the years is what "moves" me. As a student leader, I was able to participate in the preliminary discussions about the Green Music Center—from architectural designs and music to marketing and student programming—to ensure that all perspectives were taken into consideration. As a result, varying leaders throughout the nation joined efforts in making the Green Music Center a place of opportunity, world-class music, art, passion and remarkable memories. The SSU community, and those in decision-making roles, always made sure that the student experience was at the core of innovation and vision for the Green Music Center. The opportunities that the GMC would provide became the motivating factor toward success in constructing a state-of-the-art music hall.

Bridgette Dussan
Associated Students President, 2011
Sonoma State University

Philanthropy Is a State of Mind

*A*s a Sonoma State development director for many years, Robin Draper knew that bringing the Green Music Center to completion would require "many to carry the vision." That would mean having a comprehensive strategy to keep the spark alive over years of effort, as well as deal with the unexpected. "Fundraising is a day-by-day, step-by-step process," she said. "It cannot be fast-tracked. It has chapters and subchapters. It requires cultivation, marketing, commitment and patience."

There were several economic cycles and three U.S. presidential elections to come before the project was finally ready for its inaugural season. "It was the ironclad vision of the three visionary couples that kept the boat afloat," Draper remembered about the Armiñanas, Greens and Browns.

Don Green was known to say that "philanthropy is a state of mind" as he and Corrick Brown confidently took the reins of the largest capital campaign ever launched in the history of Sonoma County. Green turned to his colleagues in the high-tech industry and challenged them to raise $5 million among themselves. The industry responded with enthusiasm.

Brown worked tirelessly with his Santa Rosa Symphony committee to develop "friends" of the campaign, which would lead to significant donations. His engaging personality, commitment to the project, and connections were invaluable. The Brown family has a long history in Sonoma County, and Corrick and his wife Norma's work in getting the Green Music Center on the radar cannot be overstated. Their names opened many doors.

The Armiñanas, Greens and Browns provided initial traction. Then Barbara and Jacques Schlumberger gifted $1 million to the Santa Rosa Symphony Conductors Campaign at the very first reception, which was held in their Windsor home. John and Jennifer Webley did the same with a $1 million gift for the Symphony. Charles and Jean Schulz donated $1 million several years later to the same campaign.

By May 2001, the campaign had raised $27 million in 29 months—almost $1 million a month. Never had so much been raised in Sonoma County in such a short period. The donor honor roll showed contributions from $100 to more than $5 million.

Symphony board member Steve Carroll remembered that "every technique was employed to raise the needed funds—from one-on-one appeals to imaginative house parties, to continued receptions at Tanglewood and more."

Vice President for Development Jim Meyer pulled together his staff to take on a project that had dimensions even he had not seen before. Earlier, he had set SSU on a path of sustained fundraising that reached $26 million over five years.

The world of receptions in private homes would prove to be fertile ground leading to great rewards in the initial stages of the capital campaign. More than 100 events were hosted within a widespread geographical area over many years, creating a broader recognition and understanding of the role of SSU in the region and community.

> *Music is the great uniter. An incredible force. Something that people who differ on everything and anything else can have in common.*
>
> — Sarah Dessen, *Just Listen*

A great deal of success at these receptions came from the work of the "Three Accents," who made "house calls" throughout the North Bay for five solid years, passionately promoting the virtues of the project and its promise to the region. Armiñana, with his Cuban accent, spoke of the importance of education and performance. Green, who referred to himself as "just a kid from the Liverpool docks," spoke in his British accent of the economic boon the Center would be for business. And Brown, an American, shared his dream for the growth of the Santa Rosa Symphony. As members of the Green family, Rebecca Green Birdsall and her husband, Tom Birdsall, played an integral part in launching the project. Their commitment to the mission "for the love of music" and to their parents' legacy was strong. Tom and Rebecca also opened their home for numerous receptions

Left: From the beginning, Barbara and Jacques Schlumberger have been active supporters and friends of the Green Music Center.

Center: Corrick Brown, Donald Green and Ruben Armiñana toast the project at a gathering of friends at Lambert Bridge Winery in 2006.

Right: Jean and Charles Schulz's commitment to the project was in great part a dedication to Donald and Maureen Green, as well as their continued support of Sonoma County arts.

where the "Three Accents" painted a picture of glorious things to come. They hosted artists and dignitaries and were instrumental in drawing the right friends and neighbors to hear about the project.

"Tom and Rebecca spent many hours in the early days formulating ideas and marketing plans for the Green Music Center and for the Festival," said Marne Olson. "Their passion for the arts and intimate knowledge of the world of classical music and arts venues was invaluable."

Tours to Tanglewood continued to be offered for more than 10 years to interested donors who wanted to see where the vision had begun. More than 120 took the trip, paying their own way to experience the magic of Tanglewood. Most returned inspired to create their own "magic" at home.

Steve Carroll remembered:

"Joining President Armiñana and Santa Rosa Symphony Vice President Marne Olson at Tanglewood one summer, I saw the breathtaking extent of their magnificent vision, a campus where a dozen aspects of music were being taught simultaneously; where students could observe professional musicians rehearsing for very real concerts; where the drive for excellence was palpable and pristine. I agreed with Marne and Ruben that we could have this at SSU. We *would* have this at SSU. As I watched Marne and Ruben explore every aspect in detail of the Tanglewood operation, from the glass gift shop to ticket and trash collection, my confidence in the project became secure."

Doing a certain kind of "homework" also involved visiting the sites of many prestigious concert halls and music festivals over the years of the project, investigating operations that would enhance the "guest experience" and help the University understand the logistical issues of having such a venue on a college campus.

Olson and others remember trips to Wolf Trap, Ravinia, Avery Fisher Hall, Disney Hall, Boston Symphony Hall, Carnegie Hall and performing arts centers at other universities, to mine for inspiration. There were also trips abroad to halls in Vienna and Amsterdam.

"We took the best ideas from each place, aiming again to put a West Coast, Sonoma County spin on them," said Olson. "Everyone was so generous in sharing their initial challenges so we could do better."

Les and Judy Vadasz (top) and Anne Benedetti and family (bottom) were among the many dedicated community members who introduced the Green Music Center to their friends and neighbors.

It was a time of introduction to what would become the Green Music Center. The "three accents"—Armiñana with his Cuban accent, Corrick Brown with his American accent and Donald Green with his British accent —were invited to visit many homes to show and tell what was on the horizon.

Troubling Signs

The first signs that fundraising was starting to slow down appeared early in 2000. Don Green's red-hot telecom industry had enjoyed soaring growth thanks to the passage of the Telecommunications Act of 1996, which deregulated the industry. The technology-rich NASDAQ stock market rose dramatically from early 1997 to March 2000. Then, unexpectedly, it suffered a precipitous decline that within a year would wipe out $1 trillion of stock wealth for shareholders of telecommunications equipment manufacturers like those in Sonoma County's Telecom Valley.

Eighteen months later, with donors still reeling from the telecom crash, Al-Qaeda terrorists hijacked four commercial aircraft and flew two into the World Trade Center towers in New York City, and another into the Pentagon in Washington, D.C. Passengers sacrificed themselves to crash the fourth plane into a field in Shanksville, Pennsylvania. The September 11, 2001, crisis shook the nation to its core. Stock market exchanges closed for six days and reopened to the biggest losses in their history.

Gifts based on stock plummeted in value. Meyer acknowledged that the economy was not as bright or encouraging as it once had been. Donors lacked the confidence to increase their gifts, and new supporters were filled with doubt about both the economy and the possibility of completing the project.

During these periods, when there were few prospects on the horizon for months on end, remembering the core mission was essential to keep spirits from being extinguished for good. Olson said, "When things looked dim we remembered our mission—education—and everything seemed to lift. It was clear we had to keep the focus on that idea. Remembering it brought everything back into perspective. We could not risk becoming distracted."

Ed Stolman was one of Sonoma State University's most active "boosters" and brought his friends, colleagues and neighbors (including Joan and Sanford Weill) into the Green Music Center mix.

Generous friends, such as Stephen and Adriel Doyle, opened their homes and invited their friends to hear about the musical venue planned at Sonoma State.

Nature abhors a vacuum, and into this void marched the critics, saying the visionaries had aimed too high and reached too wide. They began to call the Green Music Center "a green elephant." The student newspaper called it "a tangled mess." Even the *Chronicle of Higher Education* questioned whether it was "a white elephant or savvy investment." The story observed, "SSU's president walks the line between needed construction and empire building." Critics also said the idea did not make sense because SSU had such a small music department.

To deal with the slowdown, in 2002 SSU decided to break the project into phases, building the main concert hall in the first phase with a price tag of $39 million.

In late 2003, holiday cheer came early as major gifts—especially a $3 million donation from Evert Person and his wife, Norma—boosted fundraising to within $1 million of the $39 million needed. And in the final weeks of that year, Santa Rosa Symphony conductors Corrick Brown and Jeffrey Kahane made up the difference with a $60,000 donation that would allow construction to begin the next year.

But then another obstacle appeared on the horizon. In 2004, the University asked contractors for bids for the first phase. They came back 35 percent over budget.

At just that time, Beijing required huge quantities of steel and concrete in preparation for the 2008 Olympics. Domestic demand in the construction industry increased prices for lumber and other wood products. California was in the midst of the greatest home-building boom in 15 years. Across the nation, the third-largest home-building rally in the last 25 years was taking place. These far-flung events converged to dramatically inflate construction costs locally.

All activity on the site stopped indefinitely. It was time to step back and rethink the project.

Back to the Future

By 2004, the Green Music Center capital campaign had raised $39 million in direct gifts and $5.25 million in deferred giving. Approximately 1,096 donors were engaged in the project, 704 of them new donors to SSU. These new contributors helped form fresh alliances and opportunities for the University, deflecting the criticism that the years of effort on behalf of the Green Music Center by the Development Office had hurt fund-raising for the academic side of the campus. In fact, it had also brought new "friends" with varied interests to the University.

The connection to Telecom Valley industries helped support the creation of the University's Master of Science in Computer and Engineering Science. Ed Stolman of Sonoma Valley, a local entrepreneur, was the spark that helped launch the Osher Lifelong

This gracious couple, Evert and Norma Person, are decades-long friends of Sonoma State University, consistently supporting performing arts students and programs, funding the Evert B. Person Theatre and investing in the Green Music Center.

Learning Institute. It was later infused with financial support by the Bernard Osher Foundation. New donors also supported numerous student scholarships, endowed funds, and ongoing academic gifts for SSU.

Despite these side benefits, costs for the Green Music Center kept ahead of the fundraising with frustrating regularity. But at a meeting in Boston in 2004 with his staff, Armiñana was presented with a new financing plan developed by Vice President Larry Furukawa-Schlereth and campus architect Bruce Walker.

"We are going back to the future, the original vision," said Armiñana, finding a silver lining. SSU announced it would revive its original plan with a $60 million multipurpose complex in a public-private partnership that proposed using $16 million in state funds for an educational wing and $7 million from Sonoma State Enterprises (an auxiliary to the campus) for what was then the conference and dining facilities (later to be called the Hospitality Center).

The CSU trustees approved the new arrangements because they were seriously impressed by the private support of the area's donors. They wanted to invest in such a public-private partnership.

The new plan allowed the concert hall and academic building to be constructed at the same time, resulting in economies of scale that would lower costs.

And finally, to offset the threat of escalating costs, the CSU approved SSU's hiring of a construction manager-at-risk (CMR), a system that involves a commitment by the construction manager to deliver the project within a guaranteed maximum price, so the bidding process would not have to be repeated. The CMR would work with the University and architect within the available budget, making adjustments to contain costs.

The future looked brighter with the prospect of tapping state educational facilities monies. SSU was making "lemonade out of lemons," said Alan Silow, Santa Rosa Symphony executive director. But a project fueled by wine entrepreneurs and a technology boom still needed to find other means of support. The search for new donors was on.

Many years after the initial vision had been sparked, there was still no construction activity at the corner of Rohnert Park Expressway and Petaluma Hill Road. A sign reading "Future Home of the Green Music Center," which had stood at the corner for years, was a constant reminder of the inability to cross the finish line.

But that was about to change.

— Jean Wasp

A University of Dreamers

It was 1999. The legendary Sonoma State University fundraiser Jim Meyer called me into his office and asked me to take a seat. He said, "I want you to begin working on a new project. You'll be fundraising for a new university concert hall."

Hold on, I thought to myself. A relatively small, budget-strapped California State University is about to launch a campaign for a 1,400-seat concert hall? Really? But then, I was a junior fundraiser, so what did I know?

Thank goodness we cannot predict the future, or even know the treacherous road ahead, the cost overruns, the highs, the lows, the ups and downs. Most of us would never begin to visualize a dream if we knew of the journey before us. And that certainly applied to the Green Music Center and Weill Hall.

The combination of the three couples—the Armiñanas, Greens and Browns—was the beginning of many chapters that unfolded and became filled with remarkable and noteworthy tales.

As we all know, the world is made up of dreamers—especially in a university. During my time at SSU, I heard a lot of dreams every day, all day long. But that's what is unique and fascinating about universities—and some of those dreams even manage to become a reality.

Robin Draper
Development Director, 1994-2009
Sonoma State University

Friendship and a Quality Center

The primary reason that Jane and I became involved in the GMC project was our friendship with Don Green. I had served on Don's Advanced Fibre Communications board and had also been an early investor in the company. We were tennis buddies as well. When he and Maureen gave the lead gift for the music center, he contacted a number of us to assist in raising the funding for it. Jane and I had a background of supporting the Santa Barbara Symphony when we lived there and were later supporters of the Santa Rosa Symphony. Adding our support to what became the Green Music Center was a good fit for us. Now, so many years later, not only is the quality of music performed in the hall impressive, but the workmanship is quite spectacular.

Herb and Jane Dwight
Entrepreneurs and Philanthropists

It really doesn't seem that long ago that every few weeks I was designing yet another custom invitation to a private gathering in a home where Don, Jeffrey and Ruben would share their vision of a world-class hall for our very own Symphony. Each invitation carried that original aerial rendering of the Green Music Center promising what could be—and we all wondered whether there was any way that such a vision could really become reality.

The price tag seemed a huge nut to crack. Yet with each passing week, as local families and individuals stepped up to the plate, opening their homes to neighbors, friends and business associates to spread the word and to learn firsthand what might be possible, the pledges grew until one day we all found ourselves standing in that grassy field to witness the first sod being turned at the groundbreaking.

Truly a remarkable experience of community coming together to create something even greater. What an incredible asset not just for our community, but for the world. And I feel so fortunate to have been part of it from its inception.

Rod Wallace
Branding and Design Consultant

It's just too bad that the name Armiñana doesn't mean vermillion or some color or another in Spanish. It would be the final perfect touch for the trio of "entertainers" who have been on the Sonoma County circuit.

The act is called Brown, Green & Armiñana; their motto is "Have Dream, Will Travel." Not since the Three Tenors started roaming the world has there been such a trio. The three are Corrick Brown, conductor emeritus of the Santa Rosa Symphony; Don Green, the "founder" of the Telecom Valley and a major contributor to the cultural life of the community; and Dr. Ruben Armiñana, president of Sonoma State University.

They've made nearly 40 "house calls" in the past months, speaking to groups of 20 or more about the proposed Green Music Center, a university complex that will include a concert hall designed by the same architects who created Ozawa Hall at Tanglewood in Massachusetts, considered to be the finest facility, acoustically, in the nation. It also will be the long-awaited home of the Santa Rosa Symphony.

Their "act" has raised $25 million and they are looking for $18 million more. They have it down pat. Ruben tells the jokes and explains how it all began when he attended a conference at Tanglewood. Corrick describes how he has perfected the art of seat-trading at Tanglewood, which has enabled him to sit in every corner of the hall, testing acoustics. Don explains how he and his wife, Maureen, came to pledge the first $10 million and points out that such a facility will be a blessing for the business community that can lure engineers and executives with the promise of a rich cultural climate.

There are no lengths to which they will not go—or at least to which Ruben will not go. Saturday at the Jonson-Ponseti (that's Stefan and Rhoann) home in Santa Rosa, the dapper little educator, in an expensive sport coat with a silk pocket handkerchief, was pacing as he talked to the group assembled by the pool.

Someone warned him to be careful not to fall in. Someone else suggested that perhaps that would be a way to raise money. He never hesitated.

For a million-dollar donation, Armiñana said, not only would he jump in the pool, but all three would perform a synchronized swimming routine. For two million, he promised, they would do it au naturel. When the resulting clamor subsided, he capitulated.

"OK, OK," he said. "For three million, we won't."

Gaye LeBaron's Notebook
The Press Democrat, October 10, 2000

JOAN & SANFORD I. WEILL HALL

If You Build It
They Will Come . . .
Eventually

The year 2005 was a turning point in both sad and wonderful ways. The project was to make significant headway but lose a favorite son in the process. Ruben Armiñana and Don Green had not given up when the going got tough. "Thank heaven for tenacity," wrote one local newspaper editor.

Armiñana was not without "helpers" who wanted to provide solutions to the ongoing financial problems. There were those who wanted him to cut costs in ways that would affect quality, but "that was not negotiable," the SSU president said. He felt that unless the quality of the experience and the acoustics were tops, there was no reason to do it. "It was always at the core of what we wanted to do. It had to be of a quality as good as, if not better than, Ozawa Hall."

That was also very important because it was not what was expected of a state institution, he said. "We wanted very much to say: Yes, we are a public institution, but we are also a quality public institution. This building is a physical statement that the high quality within the music center is the same quality occurring in the academic experience.

"Just as important is what it says to the young people watching us," the SSU president amplified. "If I am clear in my vision, if I am willing to work hard and not compromise quality, I can achieve what I set out to do. It is a statement of what can be done if you are willing to think well and work hard."

Impressive century-old olive trees line the Trione Courtyard at Weill Hall's main entrance.

Top: Community members gather in 2005 for a second ground-breaking, joining the celebration as the first pylons were about to be driven.

Bottom: Left to right, Ruben Armiñana, then-community member Dan Condron and Vice President Lynn McIntyre celebrate the second groundbreaking of the expanded Green Music Center.

Top: Floyd Ross, executive director (left), and Jeff Langley, Green Music Center artistic director, stand on the construction site of the Green Music Center happily anticipating what was to come.

Bottom: Alan Silow, executive director of the Santa Rosa Symphony, signs a steel pylon that became part of the Green Music Center's foundation at the 2005 groundbreaking ceremony.

Groundbreaking Redux

In October 2005, a second groundbreaking was held. Supporters and University officials experienced a brand-new feeling as something tangible was happening on the site for the first time.

Guests celebrated by signing one of the concrete pylons, the underground beams that support the concert hall, with good wishes. Music filled the air as musicians from the Santa Rosa Symphony and student musicians played a fanfare and anthem entitled *To All Who Come Here*, which was composed for the event by GMC Artistic Director Jeff Langley.

Speakers and distinguished guests provided celebratory comments. Don Green said, "I see a strong sense of community pride in the Green Music Center. There is an awareness that we all are creating something of lasting significance that will continue beyond our generation and beyond our community."

Soon after, bulldozers and cranes appeared on the site as construction was officially launched. An opening date of 2008 was announced. There was still $11 million to raise, but much was in place financially for the now $63 million project.

In August, the University had taken another step and worked with Live Nation to stage an Eagles concert on the SSU campus soccer fields, with 10,000 in attendance, to test how it could handle a larger event. It went surprisingly well and gave the Green Music Center planners a new understanding of parking, traffic flow, crowd control, concessions and restrooms.

As GMC programming needs loomed large, project leaders hired Ravinia Festival Director Welz Kauffman as a short-term consultant on operational issues. His insight and experience on programming was very valuable.

Then a most unexpected loss occurred. The University's chief architect, Bruce Walker, died suddenly at his home on a Sunday morning in November. He was 47, a father of two and a loving husband. In only eight years on the job as senior director for capital planning, design and construction, he had led the campus through a period that had already transformed it from its sleepy 1960s veneer into a modern university. In stepped Christopher Dinno, a University colleague and close friend, who would bring the project to completion.

Bruno Ferrandis took to the conductor's podium for the Santa Rosa Symphony in 2006.

The following year brought changes at the helm for the Santa Rosa Symphony. Jeffrey Kahane stepped down from his podium, to great acclaim and appreciation from symphony subscribers and the larger community. In his place would be Parisian Bruno Ferrandis, who was a guest conductor with orchestras all over the world but had never led his own.

Kahane was also conductor of the Los Angeles Chamber Orchestra but remained as artistic director of the Green Music Festival. Ferrandis would have the honor of conducting the Santa Rosa Symphony in the inaugural season of the Green Music Center, featuring Kahane as a guest artist.

Fundraising continued to be daunting. In 2006, $11 million still remained to be raised to complete the main concert hall. Community leaders Dan Lanahan and Jay Abbe chaired a $22 million "Finale" Capital Campaign to create new momentum for completing construction of all the facilities on the Center's grounds.

Don Green stepped into the breach again in 2007 with the idea of a Telecom Valley reunion, hoping to tap the millions recently earned by his colleagues in Telecom Valley, thanks in part to his leadership. This gesture toward these "happy days" was aimed at raising $7 million to name the main concert hall Innovation Hall. Plans were to feature an interactive display about the history of Telecom Valley in the lobby.

The night was full of tales by Telecom Valley veterans of millions made and lost, all-nighters, and last-minute hardware and software miracles. It also celebrated the 20th anniversary of the industry in the area. Fundraising continued but the $7 million goal for Innovation Hall was not met.

Left to right: Rich Stanfield, John Webley and Greg Steele, former colleagues of Don Green, at the Telecom Valley reunion in 2007.

Congresswoman Lynn Woolsey (seated) shares memories with telecom pioneers Chet and Mary Stephens and Linda Highland Johnson at the Telecom Valley reunion in 2007.

Another light emerged in Jean Schulz, wife of the late *Peanuts* cartoonist Charles Schulz, who donated $5 million for construction and was invited to name the 250-seat recital hall. Schroeder Hall, whose design is inspired by the soaring spaces of European churches, was named after the piano-playing *Peanuts* character.

Through the next few years, the recession hit and fundraising efforts sputtered no matter how creative the ideas to generate attention from donors. There were other stumbling blocks. A sewer dispute with the City of Rohnert Park seemed capable of derailing the project but was finally averted.

In 2007, Ruben Armiñana saw that his vision was only partially built and it now had a $100+ million price tag. Faculty critics became more virulent as they questioned whether campus funds had been diverted from day-to-day academic needs to support the advancement of the GMC project. They complained they were not being properly consulted about the project as it evolved. A no-confidence vote in the spring semester resulted in 450 professors and lecturers voting 73 percent to give a thumbs-down to SSU's president.

Armiñana would later say it was his darkest hour. But it was not surprising to him. Some of the same critics had once said similar things about SSU's Jean and Charles Schulz Information Center—that it was too large, too opulent, too different and too costly to build. It stands now as an example of the progressive nature of the campus.

Sonoma State architect Christopher Dinno, left, discusses the changing layout of the facility with SSU's Larry Furukawa-Schlereth, Floyd Ross, Jason Wenrick and William Rawn during a planning meeting in the late 2000s.

But nothing says "unfinished" like the lack of permanent chairs for an audience. State funding had been found in 2009 to cover the $1.7 million cost. An order was placed with the 200-year-old Fancher Chair Company for 1,400 acoustically primed chairs. It would take almost 18 months to produce and install them.

Fundraising events and hard-hat tours were held on the construction site as the main buildings in the complex began to emerge. When the concert hall was nearly finished in 2011, the fire marshall allowed 350 temporary chairs to be installed so that small events could be held to finally unveil the hall's magnificence.

After nine years of summer festivities, the Green Music Festival was put on hiatus so the University could stay focused on fundraising for the project.

The mood shifted in the summer of 2008 as the Music Department was able to begin its move from the timeworn Ives Hall to the new Music Education Hall. Most classes were held in the Center in the fall, but student ensembles continued to rehearse and perform in Ives Hall, Warren Auditorium and Person Theatre. The first student concerts were performed in the main concert hall in the fall of 2010.

There was progress on the piano front as an anonymous donor purchased a Steinway from the Steinway company and donated it to the University. This was a "C&A" piano—meaning it was reserved for "concerts" and "artists," used generally for about five years or so at top venues in the Seattle area. The very Steinway donated to SSU (#552) was one requested by Lang Lang when performing in concerts in the Seattle area.

Broadway legend Carol Channing, on a CSU fundraising tour for performing arts, gives a rendition of "Hello Dolly" with Jeff Langley accompanying on piano in SSU's Evert B. Person Theatre in 2007.

Investors in the Green Music Center attended several receptions in the completed parking lots across from the Green Music Center, taking tours and hearing about the center's bright future.

Additionally, a Fazioli grand piano was purchased by the University to complement the Steinway. Herbie Hancock had used that particular Fazioli in a Los Angeles studio; he had also played it on one of the Grammy broadcasts about three years earlier. In a flourish, Hancock autographed the soundboard before Sonoma State purchased it.

Many gestures of support surfaced periodically during these years, such as grants from the Koret and Hewlett Foundations, John and Jennifer Webley, Don and Louise Johnston (in memory of their son David Charles Johnston), the G.K. Hardt Trust and the William K. Bowes, Jr. Foundation as well as from the Santa Rosa Symphony. These gifts, and others, had a huge impact on the fundraising for the project and served to encourage others to give.

Severe cuts to higher education in California and the nation were beginning to reveal a troubling decline in public support. SSU would see its State general fund appropriations drop by 30 percent between 2007 and 2012. Hikes in tuition and other fees reached levels never seen before.

But the arrival of a couple from New York City in late 2010, who had never heard of the Green Music Center, would change the game forever and bring the vision to completion. The Fourth Accent had arrived.

— Jean Wasp

Putting a Man on the Moon in Musical Terms!

"Building a Tanglewood-like arts center in Sonoma County? Without the sponsorship of a world-renowned organization like the Boston Symphony Orchestra? Are you serious?"

Yes, those were my first words back in 1999 when I heard about the idea of building a world-class facility right here! But it did not take too long to conclude that a purpose-built performance hall might be the single most important step in strengthening the quality of music in the North Bay. And with the combined leadership of Ruben Armiñana, Corrick Brown, and Don and Maureen Green, the project looked like a slam-dunk at the time!

Well, we all know what happened thereafter! Two major economic downturns that drove costs faster than fundraising—even though the commitment to raise the resources was unwavering. As co-chair (with Dan Lanahan) of the Green Music Center Finale Campaign Committee, I know our community leaders and volunteers worked tirelessly to make it happen.

And, of course, it ultimately did! The vision was robust enough, audacious enough, inspiring enough to catch the imagination of a couple—Joan and Sandy Weill—who, though brand-new members of our county, are long-standing members of the worldwide performing arts community. A couple who immediately recognized the world-class stature of the Green Music Center. So they too joined our community and helped us make it a reality!

Jay Abbe
Co-Chair, GMC Finale Capital Campaign

Don Green asked me to lunch in Spring 2005. He told me the effort to construct the concert hall had hit a wall. Issues had arisen because of the unique structure of the project. We agreed that no model existed for this type of effort, and that numerous issues would have to be resolved. I spent a few months interviewing key players and then distributed a list of 14 issues to be resolved or put on a path to resolution. Bucky Peterson, the University Development Vice President, and the committee decided to have a widespread local campaign and at the same time concentrate on obtaining grants for naming opportunities. In early 2006, we asked Jay Abbe to serve as co-chair.

As the project increased in scale and because of inflation, costs increased. Bucky Peterson was appointed to a new CSU position and was replaced by Patricia McNeill. She was terrific to work with and elected to retire just before the opening of the hall in 2012. The goals set for the Finale Campaign were reached, and the campaign was a success, thanks to the efforts of the local community of Sonoma County.

Dan Lanahan
Co-Chair, GMC Finale Capital Campaign

A Husband's Enthusiasm

To attend the opening concert of Lang Lang at the Green Music Center was a dream come true for my family! My husband, Bruce, who passed away in 2005, was Sonoma State's Senior Director for Capital Planning, Design and Construction during the initial fundraising and planning stages of the Green Music Center. I remember several summer trips with him to Tanglewood, where he met donors from Sonoma County and the project's architects, William Rawn Associates. Bruce's excitement was contagious as he talked to me at length about the project. I immediately shared his enthusiasm after visiting Tanglewood. But it was not until attending a concert by Yo-Yo Ma in Seiji Ozawa Hall that I truly understood the

significance of having a concert hall of this caliber in Sonoma County and especially at Sonoma State University.

I thank Donald and Maureen Green and their family, as well as many other donors who had such a positive and lasting influence on my husband and his work. Bruce wanted the Green Music Center to be built as much for the Greens as he did for Sonoma County. He saw and felt their passion and love for music. He saw a truly giving couple so willing to support a project of this beauty and magnitude. We should all be thankful also to Dr. Ruben Armiñana and Larry Furukawa-Schlereth, who never gave up hope of this Center becoming a reality. What a memorable experience and honor, not only for myself, but for my two children, Melissa and Sam, to attend the opening concerts.

Therese Walker
Supporter and Friend

"Call Us When It's Built . . ."

Once Sonoma State embarked on the Green Music Center project, a small group of people—
from the campus and community—started working on publicizing it. Initially we faced many
obstacles: campus skepticism about the scope of the project, limited financial resources,
disinterest from the media. We invited members of the media and community to the campus
for many events to showcase our plans. We did market research that confirmed the viability of
the music center, but the media still kept saying to us, "Call us when it's built . . . when it's
open." It was very hard to promote something that people could not see, that did not yet exist.
After all, we only had an open field with a hole in the ground and some bales of hay to
mark the perimeter of the main hall. Once we broke ground for the music center, public interest
slowly began to change. People began to believe we actually would build a music center.
It was exhilarating to be part of the initial team for such a visionary
project. Seeing the thriving Green Music Center today, I know it was
worth overcoming the initial challenges.

Lynn McIntyre
Vice President for University Affairs, 1995-2005
Sonoma State University

5 It All Comes Together

Twenty miles from the Sonoma State University campus, across the rolling Sonoma Mountains, two East Coast transplants were settling into their new neighborhood—and would soon change the course of the project in ways never imagined.

Sanford "Sandy" Weill had made a name for himself on Wall Street as the CEO of Citigroup. He was equally well known in the music world as the longtime chairman of Carnegie Hall. His wife, Joan, had also cemented her place in the landscape of performing arts as chairwoman of the board of the Alvin Ailey Dance Foundation.

Longtime supporters of education, the Weills donated more than $1 billion of their personal fortune to institutions and nonprofits around the globe, from higher-education initiatives such as the endowment of Weill Cornell Medical College to numerous programs aimed at underprivileged youths. In 1982, Sandy Weill personally started the National Academy Foundation, with the goal of preparing young people for college and career success.

With this strong background of educational commitment and an unshakable interest in the arts, the Weills were naturally intrigued to hear from a new neighbor about the unfinished music center at nearby Sonoma State University. The late Ed Stolman— entrepreneur, avid arts supporter and longtime champion of the Green Music Center—told Joan and Sandy of a new arts center bearing a strong resemblance to the famed Seiji Ozawa Hall at Tanglewood. Ed volunteered to accompany the couple to see the unfinished complex for themselves.

After a quick drive over the rolling Sonoma hills, the Weills found themselves gazing upward at a magnificent concert hall on the northeast corner of the University campus. They were impressed—resplendent woods, picture-perfect views, and immaculate attention to detail and sound. But they needed an expert's opinion.

Pianos, like people, are sometimes even more beautiful on the inside than the outside. This photo of the inside of a Steinway shows the golden plate, strings and damper.

"It was beautifully designed—it's rare to see a concert hall with windows—but there were no permanent chairs, no lawn, no lobby," said Sandy. "We listened to staff member Kamen Nikolov play the piano, and it sounded terrific to us—but we don't have the professional ear."

So he suggested to Joan that they invite an expert to weigh in. Sandy called President Armiñana and said, "I have a friend who's going to be in San Francisco, and I'd like for him to come and see the hall and give me his opinion." He then added, "He'll be there around midnight—and his name is Lang Lang."

Friends Sanford Weill and Lang Lang share a moment that would eventually lead to Lang Lang's performance on the Green Music Center's inaugural weekend.

An internationally acclaimed pianist and a close friend of the Weills, Lang Lang made the late-night trip to the Green Music Center after a recital at Davies Symphony Hall in San Francisco. For nearly an hour, he played the Steinway on the concert hall stage, assessing the sound as the acoustic curtains were adjusted.

"I played a lot of things, from Bach to Chopin to Rachmaninoff to Beethoven," Lang Lang recalled. "For me, the hall is very similar to Tanglewood. It's really perfect."

With this vote of confidence, the Weills made their commitment: a $12 million gift to complete the hall and outdoor spaces. And a new name was bestowed upon the Green Music Center's crown jewel: the Joan and Sanford I. Weill Hall.

"We care deeply about the communities we live and work in," said Joan Weill. "When we first toured the Green Music Center we were immediately inspired by the beauty, the acoustics, and the wonderful potential for this spectacular arts venue."

The 1,400 chairs in Weill Hall complement the space whether filled with guests or sitting quietly on their own.

66

This was the long-awaited watershed moment for the Green Music Center. Construction rapidly resumed. There was a lobby to complete, lawns to landscape and a courtyard to finish along with performers' spaces, the Founders' Room, Privé and the Gallery Boardroom. An opening date for the Center was set—September 29, 2012—and programming of the inaugural season swiftly progressed.

More than 30 years at the helm of Carnegie Hall had prepared Sandy Weill for this newfound role. Robert Cole—an icon in the classical industry and the longtime director of Cal Performances at UC Berkeley—was brought in by Larry Furukawa-Schlereth, SSU's vice president for administration and finance/CFO, to lead artistic planning. With their combined experience and connections, a star-studded lineup was brought to life. Cole worked alongside Jeff Langley, then artistic director of the Donald & Maureen Green Music Center, and Furukawa-Schlereth.

Do you not know that our soul is composed of harmony?

— Leonardo da Vinci

Celebrities of the classical, vocal, jazz and world genres were called upon by Cole and the Weills. Lang Lang—whose test drive and resounding approval of the concert hall had set in motion the entire turn of events—was invited to inaugurate the Center with a grand opening concert.

An SSU student violinist entertains Maureen and Donald Green (seated) and Joan and Sanford Weill on the Weill Hall stage.

Joan and Sanford Weill are avid supporters of education, the arts and health care.

Bluegrass sensation Alison Krauss & Union Station also signed on to perform. The Santa Rosa Symphony offered a community day to introduce its subscribers to the facility. An inspirational sunrise choral concert reached for the heavens in the staging of an intimate consecration of the hall, symbolizing the many voices to come in the Hall's future.

Other headliners agreed to perform in the first season: classical superstar Yo-Yo Ma; Lang Lang; jazz great Wynton Marsalis; vocalists Barbara Cook, Joyce DiDonato and Stephanie Blythe; violin sensation Anne-Sophie Mutter; composer John Adams; Latin stars Chucho Valdés and Lila Downs, and many more. The inaugural season marched on for months, with a constant stream of renowned performers taking the stage of Weill Hall. It marked the beginning of a long and exciting road.

Final construction was completed with only days to spare, and Weill Hall and Lawn made its inaugural debut to international fanfare. The guest list was unlike anything ever seen in this quiet corner of the Wine Country.

In attendance at the inaugural gala were California Governor Jerry Brown and First Lady Anne Gust Brown, Congresswoman Nancy Pelosi, and a vast array of movers and shakers from all parts of the Bay Area. As a stunning fireworks display lit up the Sonoma skies, a new era officially began for the Green Music Center.

— Jessica Markus
Associate Director of Communications
Green Music Center

Tireless Energy and Leadership

In March 2011, the University announced a $12 million gift from Joan and Sandy Weill, who had only recently moved from New York City to Sonoma County and had never heard of Sonoma State University prior to their first visit a few months earlier. It had taken four years to raise $20 million for the Green Music Center since I arrived at Sonoma State in July 2007. Less than four months after their first visit, we had a $12 million commitment from the Weills, which would enable us to complete the concert hall and begin work on the outdoor concert space. While this was an extraordinary event, it was matched by the extraordinary dedication, commitment and generosity of the entire community over the 15 years it took to build the Green Music Center. It was a joy to work with Don and Maureen Green and their family, and the many, many other individuals whose tireless energy, leadership and boundless optimism in the face of often devastating economic conditions made it possible for this dream of a few to become a reality and blessing for many. The Green Music Center has truly become a community gathering place.

Patricia McNeill
Vice President for Development
2007-2011
Sonoma State University

A Perfect Example

The Green Music Center is stunning. It is a perfect example of how a creative vision, good planning, and perfect execution on the part of campus leadership can accomplish what at one point in time seemed like nothing more than a dream. These facilities will uplift the community, serve generations of students, and attract the attention and support of new people for Sonoma State.

Martha Walda
California State University Board of Trustees
1987-2003

6 *Construction Cliffhanger*

It was Valentine's Day in 2006 when the northeast corner of the campus began to come alive with the sights and sounds of serious construction of the Green Music Center. Workers in orange vests, earth-moving equipment, a tall crane and huge piles of building materials would cover the site for several years, reshaping it into a complex of buildings that would open up future possibilities for the community.

From the beginning of construction until the inaugural weekend in 2012, Christopher Dinno, associate vice president for capital planning, design and construction, mastered a budgetary cliffhanger that forced him to manage the complex in phases, timed to when the money could be found to allow progress.

A surprising escalation of labor and material costs of steel, copper and concrete had hit the project early and dogged the construction timeline until it was nearly finished. This was also true for all capital projects throughout the California State University system and in the state.

Dinno worked within a Construction Manager-at-Risk (CMR) partnership delivery method as part of the preconstruction, estimating, constructability reviews and construction for the project. Working closely with Rudolph and Sletten Construction and the architectural engineering team, the arrangement ensured that budgetary limitations could be overcome and construction could continue without extended delays.

The arrangement allowed the project team to solve problems as they developed early on in the process, without having to repeatedly go through a new design/bid cycle. The CMR process allowed the team to generate creative solutions and measure them against the budget at the ground level, which might not have occurred with other construction delivery methods, Dinno said.

Early groundwork on the 53-acre site had been completed before 2005 with the erection of a 190-foot-high sound berm along Petaluma Hill Road. Part of the outdoor

The orange of a worker's safety vest stands out like California poppies on a lush green field.

Frank Baroni, Rudolph and Sletten project superintendent (left), and SSU's Christopher Dinno stand on the maple stage of Weill Hall during a later construction phase and before the permanent chairs were installed.

acoustical strategy to deflect nearby road noise, it was also an attractive land feature. A new parking lot with 1,100 spaces was also built as part of the campus master plan. It was quickly put to use by the students and employees.

Building the main concert hall itself was a complex process. From tall glass windows to sound curtains, sound systems, chairs, lighting and control systems, every element was installed and then tested to ensure that the original acoustical vision was realized.

That same kind of dedication was at work in the other aspects of the Center, from Music Education Hall and Schroeder Hall to the restaurant Prelude and the beautiful landscaping that surrounded the buildings.

"Although, for a whole host of reasons, the project took longer to complete and required more money than originally expected, the glorious results came from an unfaltering dedication by everyone involved, from construction workers to donors," acoustician Larry Kirkegaard told a reporter from *Lighting & Sound America* magazine.

In expressing the remarkable outcome of the project, Dinno liked to quote Isaac Stern, who once said, "Everywhere in the world, music enhances a hall, with one exception: Carnegie Hall enhances the music."

Dinno added, "We know that there is now a second exception to this rule, and that is Weill Hall."

Design and Building Team

Design Architect
William Rawn Associates, Boston

Executive Architect
BAR, San Francisco

Executive Architect
AC Martin, Sacramento

General Contractors
Rudolph and Sletten, Inc., Foster City

Acoustical Engineer
Kirkegaard Associates, Chicago

Theatre Consultant
Auerbach Pollock Friedlander,
San Francisco

Structural Engineer
Structural Design Group, Santa Rosa
Arup, San Francisco

Mechanical Engineer
Flack + Kurtz, San Francisco
Arup, San Francisco

Electrical Engineer
Flack + Kurtz, San Francisco
Arup, San Francisco

Landscape Architect
Quadriga, Santa Rosa
SWA, Sausalito

Civil Engineer
Brelje & Race, Santa Rosa

Kitchen Consultant
Webb Design, Tustin

Hospitality Center Interior Designer
Puccini Group

Project Management –
Sonoma State University
John Bond
Christopher Dinno
Richard Marker
John Regnier
Floyd Ross
Bruce Walker

Project Management –
California State University
Pat Drohan
Stephanie Giordano
Vi San Juan

Reflections of a Romantic Notion

There is something uniquely special and timeless about grand music halls and summertime outdoor classical music concerts under the evening stars. For me, it is a romantic notion of an age of innocence and of simpler times.

I came to this extraordinary place, Sonoma State University, when the Green Music Center was just a vision, and the music program was aspiring to be the Tanglewood of the West. As an architect, I was immediately captivated by every aspect of the project and its world-class potential.

For me personally, the Grand Opening weekend was a time for reflection, as I recalled how many dedicated people had contributed their expertise to the project, and how intimately involved I had been on so many levels to get us to that moment. The celebrated milestone has been a rare opportunity to be part of a history with which I am so blessed and grateful to be associated.

Sir Winston Churchill said: "We shape our buildings; thereafter they shape us."

The notion of the "age of innocence" is alive and well at Sonoma State University and the Green Music Center; the vision, venue, this place—we can all relate to it for the way it makes us feel. This journey has been deeply nostalgic and makes me keenly aware of the privilege of being part of something uniquely special.

Christopher Dinno

Associate Vice President for Administration and Finance
Facilities Operations and Planning
Sonoma State University

Flying High Above

One day when I was on an assignment shooting construction photos at the Green Music Center site, the crane operator, Ron, saw me with my camera from his perch high up in the crane. He offered me a photo opportunity of a lifetime.

This required getting in a little cage up front of the crane. Ron would sit in his captain's chair and up, up, up we would go for a 360-degree view. My site visits revealed that each job required a master craftsperson.

A keen level of respect grew from watching the skill and expertise of the workers. Impressive all—from Ron, the crane operator, who would lift huge beams suspended on wires into place, to a man who reminded me of Hercules. A beam would be flown in on the crane and the other workers stood back while Hercules went up to the pylon, wrapped his arms around it, and guided it into place. Another day, I watched the tile guy carefully hand-cut each tile for the exterior of Schroeder Hall. He would pass it off to the other guys, who would go put it in place, then move on to the next brick. There were so many moments like this, all captured in the photos I took.

The Green project took me down so many alleyways, twists and turns, people and places from all over Sonoma County. Let my images tell part of the story and give you a glimpse into a journey that has taken 15 years to create.

Linnea Mullins
University Photographer

Building a Cathedral

The Donald and Maureen Green Music Center and Joan and Sanford I. Weill Hall represent a truly transformational leap for Sonoma County and the North Bay. There is no turning back now.

What does this mean for the economy and our community? It means companies that value having a vibrant arts scene available to their employees will know that Sonoma County has indisputably one of the finest music halls in the world. It means the University could become a center of music innovation where the seeds of new companies are planted.

On the broadest level, the center is a gift for the ages to the community— ensuring that the best music human beings can create will have a performance venue equal to their talents.

The few times I toured Weill Hall when it was under construction I thought to myself, "Even the construction sounds like music." Like the self-aware stonecutter who knows he is not merely cutting stone but is building a cathedral, the trades- and craftspeople and other professionals seemed to know they were building something very special.

They did build it. And we will all be the beneficiaries for decades to come.

Brad Bollinger
Publisher, North Bay Business Journal

Execution Meets Expectations

The design of the Green Music Center was stunning and the execution even better. The CSU Trustees were well taken with it from the beginning and enthusiastically supported it.

The execution met expectations that were very high. Years of fundraising—and consciousness-raising about its importance—resulted in a physically beautiful and significant building on a popular campus of the CSU.

Richard West

CSU Executive Vice Chancellor

1994-2008

SSU Professor of Economics

Starting with only a vision and a mission (Aim high. Reach wide. Educate all.), the Green Music Center rose from the ground—beneath the ground in the case of Weill Hall—to grow into the majestic creation it is today.

The effort of creating this community gem involved individuals with talents in many areas, and work spanning several years. While the construction was under way, hundreds of interested community members toured the buildings and participated in outdoor receptions and gatherings. All were striving toward the same goal.

7 *Inside/Outside*

Weill Hall: An Adventure into Acoustics and Architecture

*B*uilding a great concert hall is an act of courage and determination.

Floyd Ross, the first executive director of the Green Music Center project, who made his way around the world investigating the attributes of successful halls, eventually came to the conclusion that the world of architectural acoustics is "10 percent science and 90 percent magic."

"Millions of dollars have been spent by experienced professionals who attempt to build a concert hall that eventually fails," said Ross. "And often, it is not known until opening night if the acoustical design has succeeded. A hall that fails on opening night can be scarred for years. Bad publicity has a habit of lingering long after the problems have been fixed."

But this did not happen at Ozawa Hall at Tanglewood, nor later at Weill Hall at Sonoma State University. At both halls, the "shoe-box" design delivered and world-class halls were born.

At Tanglewood, the owners were looking to replace a dilapidated wooden structure called the Music Theatre that had been used for music student training and occasional concerts. The floor was dirt and the seats were uncomfortable.

Known for supporting and encouraging emerging musical artists and not afraid to move from the conventional, the Tanglewood committee chose an architect who was known for his affordable-housing projects but had never built a concert hall. Competing with 40 other colleagues, Bill Rawn and his poignant commentary on the importance of "place" in a building project enthralled the committee, and he was awarded the contract. He said he imagined the new hall appearing on the landscape as "a brightly lit lantern" that one comes upon while strolling the Tanglewood grounds.

Many fine pieces of art, donated, purchased or on loan, grace the interior and exterior of the Green Music Center. The art serves to complement the music and education center.

The hall project came together easily, on time and on budget. At Bill Rawn's office, it was often referred to as "the affordable music hall." Built for $10 million over four years, it was completed in 1994. It has been named second best in the United States and fourth best in the world in the past 50 years by Leo Beranek in his acoustical survey, *Concert Halls and Opera Houses: Music, Acoustics, and Architecture*. Rawn often cites the importance of Larry Kirkegaard's work in this recognition of the hall's acoustics.

In his opening night review on July 7, 1994, *New York Times* music critic Edward Rothstein said about Ozawa, "It is exactly what a concert hall should be . . . a resonant, warm space that comes to life with sound."

The first music hall that Bill Rawn designed was a home run. So when Ruben Armiñana and Marne Olson experienced it, they decided that SSU should take advantage of Ozawa's success by bringing in the same architect and acoustician to replicate it on the SSU campus. Why risk failure when success is so attractively available? Sixteen long years later, the hall opened to a standing ovation.

The Hall as an Instrument

The 1,400-seat Weill Hall is designed in the "shoe-box" style of Ozawa Hall, with balconies along both sides and both ends wrapping around the entire hall. Weill Hall carries the DNA of Ozawa, but it is not a clone. There are many differences that set the two apart. The Weill Hall mission, as part of a state university campus, was to provide for a year-round operation. From the start, the vision was for the entire Green Music Center to be a place where the world of arts and ideas could thrive, where the next generation of fine musicians, vocalists and dancers could develop their artistry.

[Weill Hall] is so well balanced with natural light and wood finishes that it glows a honey color. Unbelievably beautiful building. Made almost entirely from maple and alder railings, chairs, paneling. Acoustically rich and personal for an auditorium. This building will be loved by the public for centuries.

— Daniel Nichols, *Architect Magazine*

Ozawa Hall was designed as an interpretation of a New England meetinghouse, given its location in the Berkshires, with so many such buildings on town greens nearby. Ozawa's roof derived from a Shaker tradition, namely the curved roof of the workshop building in the Mount Lebanon Shaker Village in New Lebanon, New York. That roof was meant to respond to the rolling hills surrounding a nearby lake, Stockbridge Bowl. Ozawa is a very inward-focused building, with limited glimpses out through glass doors to the green trees of the

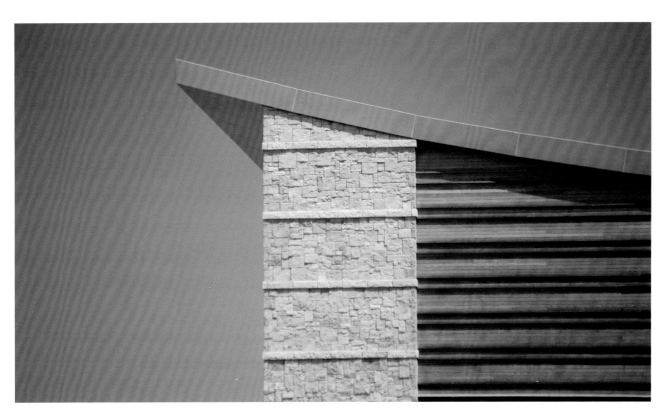

site as well as a view of the sky. The hall itself has strong vertical motifs. It has 1,200 seats and is a perfect "double square" in shape, meaning it is twice as long as it is wide.

Weill Hall, in contrast, has more seats and is slightly narrower and definitely longer than Ozawa. This gives the room a much stronger horizontal nature. And in all the detailing—wood, window slats, balcony finish—that horizontality is accentuated. Even more important is the opening of a huge wall of windows facing the hills to the east. From most of the seats, audience members have the panorama effect of serene mountains.

"My personal sense of Californian sensibilities joined with the open, often dry California landscape to shape this strong connection to the land through those windows facing east to the landscape," said Rawn.

Weill Hall has a high western roof edge that sweeps down and gives a hint of responding to the upward slope of the hills to the east. "We like to think this roof form nestles the building into the valley," said Rawn. "This valley orientation is distinctly different from Ozawa, which celebrates the gentle rounded hilltops of the Berkshires."

Bill Rawn's philosophy is always to put people together in a democratic fashion, so that they "rub shoulders with one another." The space itself is warm and inviting. Upon entry, it feels like an outdoor cathedral with wooden garden chairs.

The beauty of Weill Hall can be seen in every aspect of its design, including the floors, ceiling, banisters and chairs. Every piece was reviewed for its enhancement to the acoustics and aesthetics of the hall.

The balconies surrounding all sides of the hall, including the back of the stage, are designed so people can see each other enjoying performances and thus have a shared experience. A sense of community is created when a portion of the audience sits along the side walls and around the stage. This seating also puts the audience closer to the performers. Rawn likes to place people where they can see the "whites of the eyes of everyone around them."

Rising 53 feet from the stage to the ceiling, and spanning 53 feet across from balcony to balcony and 75 feet from the face of the rear balcony to the front of stage, the nearly five-story building has the height and narrowness necessary to provide acoustical excellence for the number of people sitting in the hall. Because sound waves like curves, the interior side walls lean outward three degrees from the back of the stage to the back of the hall.

Why It Works

Being inside Weill Hall is very much like being inside a musical instrument, one that naturally amplifies and enriches every note that is played. "One of the things the ear likes to hear is reflected sound coming really, really close to the direct sound. It gives a sense of intimacy and contact," said acoustician Larry Kirkegaard, who collaborated with architect Bill Rawn to develop the acoustical excellence in both Ozawa and Weill Halls. "You want the sound to embrace you like a warm hug."

As rooms get wider or taller, the time it takes sound to go out and come back to the listener gets more and more delayed. "Some of that desired intimacy begins to feel at arm's length. So the narrowness of a hall is a very, very good thing," said Kirkegaard. "Everywhere in the hall you sense the closeness of the audience; you feel the warmth and excitement of everyone around you."

"The natural acoustics of the place are like what a fresh clean canvas must be to a great artist," said Patrick Maloney, a sound engineer who gave many tours of Weill Hall as it was being completed. Maloney currently serves as director of guest services at the Green Music Center. "There is nothing to overcome, nothing to fight, in order to get intelligible sound into the back corners and far reaches of the balcony."

acoustics

The acoustic design of the 1,400-seat, shoebox-shaped Green Music Center's concert hall is designed to rival great halls such as Boston Symphony Hall and Vienna Musikvereinssaal. It embodies the acoustical attributes of Seiji Ozawa Hall at Tanglewood; however, it surpasses its predecessor in terms of flexibility and comfort, while reducing its operating carbon footprint.

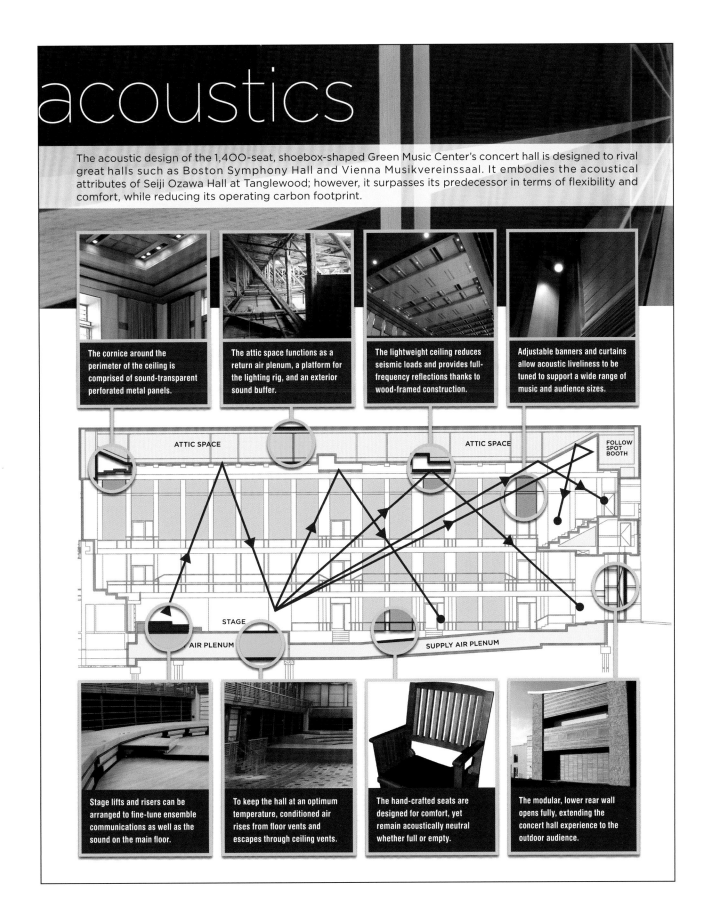

The cornice around the perimeter of the ceiling is comprised of sound-transparent perforated metal panels.

The attic space functions as a return air plenum, a platform for the lighting rig, and an exterior sound buffer.

The lightweight ceiling reduces seismic loads and provides full-frequency reflections thanks to wood-framed construction.

Adjustable banners and curtains allow acoustic liveliness to be tuned to support a wide range of music and audience sizes.

Stage lifts and risers can be arranged to fine-tune ensemble communications as well as the sound on the main floor.

To keep the hall at an optimum temperature, conditioned air rises from floor vents and escapes through ceiling vents.

The hand-crafted seats are designed for comfort, yet remain acoustically neutral whether full or empty.

The modular, lower rear wall opens fully, extending the concert hall experience to the outdoor audience.

ATTIC SPACE

ATTIC SPACE

FOLLOW SPOT BOOTH

STAGE

AIR PLENUM

SUPPLY AIR PLENUM

Wood Works

Every architectural element makes an acoustic contribution as well as an aesthetic and structural one. Rawn and Kirkegaard believe there is a profoundly memorable experience in a hall when the audience can literally touch the warmth of the wood.

There are four major types of wood used in Weill Hall: maple, Douglas fir, European steamed beech and cedar. Each one contributes its own unique and resonant characteristics to the overall sound.

The stage is constructed of hard maple and acts like a sounding board to project the sound of the performers out into the hall. The maple surfaces are mounted onto cross layers of thick, high-quality plywood that in turn are supported by small neoprene squares. This makes the stage's surface quite strong and rigid, and yet it floats like a membrane that supports the music being performed upon it, almost like the back of a fine stringed instrument.

The audience floor area is made of Douglas fir and has a density close to that of the spruce typically used for the top or front of better-quality stringed instruments.

Most of the other wooden surfaces, such as the railings and other trim pieces, are made from rich European steamed beech. The underside of the side balconies consists of cedar planks with beveled edges that reflect and diffuse the sound coming from the stage.

Most notable is the balcony railing design. Not only do the individual cross-members keep a guest from taking a tumble, but they are spaced apart in slightly different distances that are barely noticeable. The acoustic result is that sound from the stage bounces off each piece at a slightly different angle. This creates a scattered and diffuse reflection. Many horizontal and vertical wooden pieces serve to reflect and diffuse the sound to create a rich and even aural field.

Windows

Patrons seated on the west side of the hall have a glorious view of Sonoma Mountain. Weill Hall is a rich golden color, and those who attend concerts at various times of the day are treated to a beautiful light show as the sun moves across the sky. In the evening, the windows above the stage are filled with an ever-darkening sky as it turns from blue to black over the mountain range.

Sliding Rear Door

An innovative sliding wall at the rear of the hall came out of the culture of Tanglewood as a "happy occurrence" that became an integral part of the Weill Hall design, said Kirkegaard. The panelized door system is 20 feet high and 54 feet wide and runs the entire width of the south wall. When opened, it extends the reach of the concert hall to an additional 4,094 patrons on the Weill Lawn and Terrace outside.

Acoustic Curtains

Long, gorgeous reverberations are not appropriate for certain types of music, so in order to accommodate a wide range of musical styles, as well as lectures and spoken-word performances, computer-controlled acoustic curtains are installed on every level of the hall—a gift of the Santa Rosa Symphony. They can be deployed to various lengths to specifically tailor the amount of reverberation needed.

Sitting Pretty – A "Made in America" Story

In a concert hall, comfortable seating is as important as the acoustics. Each of the 1,400 European steamed beech chairs in Weill Hall was ergonomically designed to optimize acoustics.

Fabricating each of the 1,400 chairs was done with expertise and care.

Installing them was an intensive project that took many weeks.

The design of the handcrafted chairs is based on a comfortable garden chair and complements the look of the concert hall. Each unit was manufactured for its own unique spot on the main concert hall floor or in the balconies and is an important part of the acoustical design of the hall.

The chairs took three to four months to produce. Much of the work was done by hand by the artisans at the 200-year-old Fancher Chair Company in Falconer, New York. Each is fitted with a maroon cushion. The chairs are distinctive because they represent a rare combination of traditional wood mortise-and-tenon joinery with a functional and unique tip-up seat.

Christopher Dinno, associate vice president for capital planning, design and construction, oversaw the complex management of the project with a special team comprised of an ergonomist, acoustician, architect and theater consultant. The design is based on the ergonomic work of Mary Christiansen of Seating Dynamics, who developed the chairs for Ozawa Hall at Tanglewood. What was produced after many rounds of testing are chairs that provide patrons with a feeling of richness, comfort and accessibility.

There are multiple variations of the chair, depending on where it is anchored to the floor—from individual chairs to groups of two to three joined together. Seats along aisles open with a gate on the side to accommodate wheelchair users and those with seating challenges. Some 1,300 are anchored to the floor. Second-row chairs in the first balcony are taller to allow for good sight lines to the stage. Some chairs in the balconies are loose to enable more flexibility of arrangement. Aisle seats are equipped with special lighting.

Coordinating the production and installation of the chairs was Theatre Solutions, Inc., a manufacturer from Pennsylvania that specializes in providing custom installations of fixed seating.

What makes a concert hall "world class"?

It must be so quiet that the very soft (pp) passages are clearly audible. It must have a reverberation time long enough to carry the crescendos to dramatic very loud (ff) climaxes. The music must be sufficiently clear that rapidly moving violin passages do not melt into a general "glob." The hall should have a spacious sound, making the music full and rich and apparently much "larger" than the instrument from which it emanates. It must endow the music with a pleasant "texture" . . . The bass sounds of the orchestra must have "power" to provide a solid foundation to the music. Finally, there should be no echoes or "source shift."

— Leo Beranek, in *Concert Halls and Opera Houses: Music, Acoustics, and Architecture*

Weill Lawn and Commons

The Joan & Sanford I. Weill Lawn and Commons were designed as a landscape similar to a Northern California coastal ecosystem. Visitor-friendly "meadows" are broken up by red oak and redwood trees with extensive areas of understory planting, ground cover and mulch.

The lawn lies to the south of Weill Hall and covers 78,500 square feet. Terraced levels feature table seating for 1,648 (at 388 tables) and lawn seating for an additional 2,446 (total of 4,094 outside) and allow the concert experience to extend beyond the walls of Weill Hall. The Weill Commons is adjacent to the Weill Lawn and is an additional outdoor space adaptable for multiple events and activities for up to 10,000 patrons.

Koret Grand Entry

Through a generous gift from the Koret Foundation, a beautiful walkway was created, welcoming guests to the facility and leading them toward both the Ticket Center and the Trione Courtyard.

Trione Courtyard

The elegant Trione Courtyard, a gift of Eileen and Henry Trione, is a key component of the Green Music Center. The courtyard is framed by a stone colonnade. The traditional heavy timber wood canopy cover has a walking surface of random-pattern amber gold flamed finished stone.

Lining the courtyard are elegant and majestic 118-year-old heritage olive trees. These 12 old-growth Sevillano trees were personally selected by Joan and Sandy Weill from the Heritage Olive Trees orchard, run by Troy Heathcote in Northern California. The trees immediately took to their new location and offer visitors a unique close-up view of ageless beauty. With their silver-gray leaves and their twisted and gnarled trunks, they are an architectural and artistic statement.

The old-growth olive trees that line the Trione Courtyard create a natural outdoor meeting space before and after performances.

Person Lobby

The Person Lobby, a gift of Evert and Norma Person, is immediately adjacent to
Weill Hall and the Trione Courtyard and is the first indoor space most guests experience
as they enter the Green Music Center. It is a large, grand space of stone flooring,
beautiful chandeliers, a sweeping staircase to the upper levels, and windows looking out
to the Trione Courtyard and the beautiful Sonoma landscape to the south. Not only
does the space serve as a grand entrance to Weill Hall, it is itself a venue. Many events
such as receptions, meetings and other types of mid-sized gatherings take place in the
Person Lobby.

The beautiful Person Lobby, with stone floors and windows facing into the hall, is an engaging place for guests to gather during intermission.

Schroeder Hall – A Stage for All Seasons

Inspired by the soaring spaces of European churches, the 3,420-square-foot Schroeder Hall is notable for its curved architecture, soaring ceilings and dedicated loft for a 1,248-pipe Brombaugh Opus 9 tracker organ.

Named by philanthropist and community leader Jean Schulz in recognition of her late husband's piano-playing *Peanuts* character, Schroeder Hall features seating for 250 in a cathedral-like building, tall and thin, designed to accentuate melodic voice and instrumental music as it moves throughout the hall. The walls have been constructed with no

Schroeder Hall is not only a venue for smaller performances, but is also used as a classroom for the music and many other departments on campus.

90-degree angles to aid in the flow of sound and bring it to the ear of the listener in exactly the way it was intended to be heard. The Hall is designed to support a wide range of music from Monteverdi and Bach to works by contemporary composers. While it is intended primarily for instrumental recitals, choral music and pipe organ music, the Hall accommodates jazz combos and multimedia lectures as well.

"Few venues afford such flexibility while maintaining an intimate feel," said Jeff Langley, former artistic director of the Green Music Center. "Schroeder Hall is a space where new artists and new works can be presented, providing a great diversity of repertories to the students of SSU. Beyond performance, the building will wonderfully accommodate master classes, conferences and intellectual exchanges that engage all academic disciplines."

The colonnade, gifted by Don and Louise Johnston in honor of their son David, is a pathway to Prelude restaurant and the Dwight Courtyard Gallery, where fine works of art adorn the walls.

Designed by BAR Architects of San Francisco, Schroeder Hall is also utilized as an expanded classroom for the University, becoming one of the largest academic spaces on campus. The music department produces more than 60 annual performances, many of which take place in Schroeder Hall. The wider community has also found a home at Schroeder Hall, with events being held there on a regular basis.

James David Christie, Boston Symphony organist and one of the world's great organists, stands beside the gorgeous Brombaugh Opus 9 organ installed in Schroeder Hall.

An Organ in a Jewel Box – The Brombaugh Opus 9

Every musical space needs a centerpiece, something for the audience to gaze upon. If the centerpiece is also a source of magnificent sound, so much the better. In the Green Music Center's Schroeder Hall, that centerpiece is an exquisite Brombaugh Opus 9 tracker organ located above the stage—a wonderful gift made possible by generous donations from B.J. and Bebe Cassin, Donald and Maureen Green, and Bob Worth and Margaret McCarthy.

"The combination of Brombaugh's Opus 9 and Schroeder Hall will create a space unrivaled in the Bay Area," said Bob Worth, retired SSU choral director and faculty advisor in the long search for the right organ for the Green Music Center. "Perfect for early music, chamber music, choral and solo vocal music, and also for folk, acoustic jazz and world music, Schroeder Hall will quickly become a destination for those seeking an intimate musical experience."

The music from this instrument exhibits both exceptional clarity and warmth, said Charles Rus, an organist and consultant for the purchase of the Brombaugh Opus 9. "The colors of the sound are unusually brilliant, and the hall is perfect for it."

Crafted particularly to carry the sounds of a Buxtehude prelude, a Bach fugue or a Handel organ concerto, the instrument is also versatile enough to play many earlier and later styles. It is the ninth in a series of 66 built by the landmark American organ builder John Brombaugh. He derived his unique organ designs from extensive research into the 400-year history of European organs from the Baroque era throughout Germany and the Netherlands.

Brombaugh's Opus 9, built in 1972 for a Baptist church in Toledo, Ohio, is a mechanical-action organ that supplies air to 1,248 pipes ranging in size from 16 feet long to some smaller than a pencil. Built of red oak with accents of rare woods, the organ has metal pipes that were hand-poured, a rarity for these times. With two keyboards and a pedal board, the instrument has 20 stops and 29 ranks. There is 24-karat gold leaf on some of the pipes.

"With this instrument we could get an organ culture going here," mused Rus, "or maybe even an organ department. Though not exceptionally large, it has a full and powerful sound. It will make people love organ music!"

The entrance to Music Education Hall leads to the lobby, Schroeder Hall, practice rooms, ensemble rooms and instrument storage.

Music Education Hall

It would be easy to say that the GMC's Music Education Hall is just a building, but that is not quite accurate. Since the Department of Music began its transition in 2008 from its longtime home in Ives Hall, the sound of construction equipment has given way to the overtones of a concert or rehearsal or lesson in progress.

Melodic notes from pianos, concertos and jazz music from music appreciation courses, and other music fill the air. Groups of students rehearse together in ensemble and rehearsal rooms.

Music Education Hall is neatly divided into classrooms and practice and rehearsal rooms on the ground floor, and offices, conference rooms and a student lounge on the second floor. The lounge, situated strategically in the middle of the top floor, is a true agora, or meeting place, where students catch up on homework, eat lunch, lasso a passing professor or simply hang out.

Professor Doug Leibinger makes use of one of Music Education Hall's larger practice rooms to work with SSU's jazz ensemble.

SSU's music students played their first public performance in the Green Music Center's Weill Hall in 2010. "Like the shuffle on your iPod" was how Music Department Chair Dr. Brian S. Wilson described it. "Hold your applause" until the end, he instructed. "I guarantee that this will be a breathtaking, spectacular sensory overload."

On stage were the University Chorus, Symphonic Wind Ensemble and Jazz Orchestra Brass Ensemble, String Orchestra, Latin Band, operatic and jazz vocal soloists, Guitar Ensemble, chamber musicians, Chamber Wind Ensemble and Clarinet Choir.

The program of 18 selections lasted just one hour and moved seamlessly from one performance to the next. It was met with long and resounding applause from the appreciative audience.

The synergy and excitement of the evening was felt by the music students as well as the audience. "This is our lab. This is where we practice our art," said Lynne Morrow, SSU music professor.

Christopher Mauger was a senior with a double major in jazz studies and composition when he first performed in Weill Hall. "I started out as a physics major. I took a semester off from physics and took some music classes and realized how much there is to learn about music," said Mauger. "What I really like about the program is how open everyone is to what you want to do. I can compose the music that I want, not music in somebody else's style."

Labs for Learning – What's Inside

Music program classes, rehearsals, performances and other activities that take place in Music Education Hall include pianos in every classroom, rehearsal space and practice studios. Key elements include:

- Student Practice Suite and the Music Education Hall Arcade – a gift of Leslie and Judy Vadasz that is comprised of a state-of-the-art "smart" classroom that supports a variety of electronic media for PowerPoint, audio, video presentation and online services
- Soundproof teaching studios and three practice rooms
- Designated instrument storage room with locking instrument cabinets
- Large rehearsal room (2,300 square feet)
- Small rehearsal room (1,200 square feet)
- Music library (a gift of Arnie and Gayle Carston)
- Student lounge (a gift of Robert Gilchrist)
- Wireless access
- Keyboard lab including 13 Yamaha Clavinova digital keyboards (a gift of Harry and Maggie Wetzel)

Artworks

Rather than thinking of art and nature as opposite forces to be balanced, I see them as parallel forces seeking equilibrium. Art and nature, yin and yang, East and West, object and idea, science and spirit, the universe and our own life force.

— Bruce Johnson, Sculptor

Bruce Johnson spent two days bolting together the pieces of his majestic redwood-and-copper iconic sculpture *Asia, 2000* to stand on the grounds of the Green Music Center. It was the first piece of outdoor sculpture to arrive before the inaugural weekend, when thousands would see it for the first time. Installed across from Music Education Hall, it is one of many exciting new works that are part of a new era of public art on campus.

No doubt the crane and construction workers were helpful, as this popular public work is 33 feet high and 33 feet wide and includes a lintel and two grand columns leaning toward each other.

This "sacred portal," as Johnson calls it, is designed with richly worked copper detailing. The textured wood columns rise with force from the grounded copper base. The whole piece stands as an "inspired gateway between ancient columns to the world of nature."

"It's been gratifying to have the support of our growing group of generous donors who have made the art at the Green Music Center possible, and exciting to see the work arrive, piece by piece," said Michael Schwager, professor of art history and a member of the Campus Art Committee.

Asia, 2000 was a signature outdoor sculpture at Paradise Ridge Winery in Santa Rosa, a gift of Dr. Walter Byck, who had the piece displayed from 2002 until 2012 in Marijke's Grove, an outdoor sculpture garden named after his wife. He then donated *Asia, 2000* to the Green Music Center, again in memory of his wife.

Welcoming patrons as they arrive at the box office to pick up their tickets is Stephen De Staebler's *Winged Figure Ascending, 2011*. It is not surprising that De Staebler, a Bay Area artist of international repute who died in 2011, created works that emanate spiritual transcendence as well as fragility and resiliency.

Just inside the Koret Grand Entry sits Stephen De Staebler's inspiring sculpture *Winged Figure Ascending, 2011*, welcoming guests as they arrive.

After De Staebler had received a degree in religion from Princeton, his own personal journey led him to later earn a Master of Fine Arts degree from the University of California at Berkeley and go on to a career that transformed the craft of ceramics. His mastery over the years helped elevate thinking about clay to more ambitious themes.

De Staebler lived and worked in Berkeley and taught for many years at San Francisco State University. His work, which is primarily figurative yet not traditional in its depiction of the human form, is in private and public collections throughout the country.

This sculpture is on loan from De Staebler's estate, as is a second work entitled *Figure with Sandstone Head, 2010*. Standing 71 inches tall, it is made of stoneware and earthenware, and is installed in the lobby of Music Education Hall.

What more perfect location to place the *Bar Note Bench* than just outside Schroeder Hall, named for the piano-playing *Peanuts* character. Sitting is philanthropist and long-term friend Jean Schulz.

Setting a humorous tone for Music Education Hall is Robert Ellison's *Bar Note Bench*, a 900-pound steel bench that joins four upward-pointing 16th notes by a double beam. Donated by Jean Schulz, wife of the late *Peanuts* cartoonist Charles Schulz, *Bar Note Bench* had originally been on display at the Paradise Ridge Winery in Santa Rosa. Schulz admits she loved it on sight and thought it evoked memories of Schroeder, the piano-playing *Peanuts* character—a place perhaps to take a break after a serious session of practicing Beethoven on his diminutive toy piano.

Along with the Ellison and Johnson sculptures, a major work by noted Sonoma County painter Jack Stuppin has also been donated to SSU and is displayed in the Founders' Room of the Green Music Center. Titled *Alexander Valley and St. Helena, 2004*, the oil-on-canvas painting measures 63 by 84 inches and portrays the beautiful landscape of the North Bay. Stuppin was for many years a member of the *plein air* painting group the Sonoma Four, and his work has been displayed nationally in many solo and group exhibitions.

All of the Green Music Center artwork was selected by community members and donated to SSU specifically to be installed on the grounds around the Center. In addition, the University, through the generosity of private donors, has purchased five photographs by the renowned photographer Wolfgang Volz depicting Christo and Jeanne-Claude's legendary outdoor artwork *Running Fence: Sonoma and Marin Counties, 1972-76*.

The large-scale images are displayed in the Dwight Courtyard Gallery, a gift of Herb and Jane Dwight. As guests walk to Weill Hall through the Gallery, they encounter beautiful images that document different stages of the Christo project. From its start atop Meacham Hill in Penngrove to its dramatic descent to the Pacific Ocean in Bodega, it ran a distance of 24½ miles. Framing for these striking photographs was made possible in part by the support of My Daughter the Framer in Santa Rosa.

A number of SSU students and faculty participated in the installation of *Running Fence* in 1976, and the photographs serve as a link between Sonoma County's new world-class performing arts facility and the world-class visual art event that took place in the area decades earlier.

"In the coming years, we hope to bring even more high-quality artwork to the Green Music Center and to the rest of the SSU campus," said Schwager. "These wonderful initial contributions are only the beginning of an environment created that stimulates an appreciation for the arts among the campus community and visitors to SSU."

The brilliantly colored painting by Jack Stuppin adds brightness and color to the Dwight Courtyard Gallery.

Hospitality Center

The Hospitality Center is adjacent to Weill Hall, accommodating not only concertgoers before, during and after most performances, but also private rentals throughout the year. Comprised of a fine-dining restaurant, outdoor spaces and three multifunctional rooms, the Hospitality Center is a popular location for weddings, meetings and special events.

Left: Prelude restaurant's patio, with fire pits and a water feature, draws diners and others out to enjoy Sonoma County evenings.

Center: The bar in Prelude is a nice place to start an evening's experience in Weill Hall.

Right: Prelude restaurant features exemplary culinary creations with exquisite attention to detail. The bright and flavorful menu will pull from the bounty of locally grown foods from Sonoma County.

Prelude restaurant anchors one end of the Hospitality Center, consisting of an elegant dining room, full bar and spacious patio. The chefs and kitchen staff produce exemplary culinary creations with seasonal menus focused on locally sourced products. Connected to the restaurant is a luscious event lawn, making Prelude an ideal location for Wine Country weddings.

Just next door to Prelude is Privé, a space ideal for business meetings or intimate events. With a full audio-visual package and access to all of the restaurant's amenities, Privé is a popular location for conference groups and campus meetings, and can accommodate more than 70 guests.

Completing the Hospitality Center are the Founders' Room and the Gallery Board Room, additional spaces for a wide range of private events. The Founders' Room features a built-in bar and access to Weill Hall's backstage areas. A popular meeting space during concerts and events, the Founders' Room is also available for private rentals.

The Gallery Boardroom, designed by Christopher Dinno, is an intimate but exquisite space, and houses the Center's wine collection in stately wooden cabinets. Ideal for groups of 20 or fewer, this space is well suited for a private dinner beneath the room's enchanting chandeliers.

— Jean Wasp

The Hall as an Instrument

For a music degree, the private lesson is the most critical piece; it leads directly to a person's ability to perform. The music department gives voice and instrumental music students the opportunity most Wednesdays to have repertory classes in Weill Hall. Every week, six or seven students sing what they are working on in their private lessons, in the hall. As I said several years ago, the concert hall is our lab. It's where we can experiment with our performing and listening skills. As performers who use and create sound, we need to have a performing space that is responsive in order to learn about what we're doing—and the hall is that instrument. You can't do that in a practice room.

These repertory classes are crucial for student learning. Another critical element is created when the students are able to attend concerts given by professionals in the concert hall. In order to become an artist—to understand what being a professional is all about—you have to see it, hear it, and experience it.

Our students have had the opportunity to have direct contact with artists such as Barbara Cook, Stephanie Blythe and Wynton Marsalis after their concerts. These are some of the wonderful opportunities we've had so far to broaden the music education of our students at Weill Hall and the Green Music Center.

Dr. Lynne Morrow
Professor of Music
Sonoma State University

Santa Rosa Symphony
Takes Its Place as Resident Orchestra

*A*fter many years of discussions, fundraising, meetings, planning, construction—and excitement—the 84-year-old Santa Rosa Symphony proudly settled into its home as Resident Orchestra of the Green Music Center.

Founded in 1928, it is the third-oldest and seventh-largest professional orchestra in California, and the largest regional symphony north of Los Angeles. Bruno Ferrandis is the fourth Music Director/Conductor in the organization's history. His predecessors were Jeffrey Kahane (1995-2006), Corrick Brown (1957-1995), and George Trombley (1928-1956).

In 2003, the Symphony's board of directors set a strategic course with a new, bold vision: to become one of the leading regional symphony orchestras in America— a model for artistic excellence, community engagement and fiscal vitality. No one envisioned the great recession of 2008 and its aftermath, as so many orchestras across the country faced increasing deficits, cuts in their services, and in some painful cases, strikes and bankruptcies. Yet this orchestral organization persevered, and has not only survived but also thrived.

Symphony Executive Director Alan Silow has played a leadership role since 2002, having produced an operating-budget surplus for 10 years that has resulted in expanded offerings for the community and a sustainable budgetary growth of 58 percent, to nearly $4 million, as well as an endowment growth of more than 300 percent, to $6.5 million.

In 2000, with Marne Olson as their board chair, the Santa Rosa Symphony forged a partnership with Sonoma State University to bring world-class music to the North Bay and provide a permanent performance home for the orchestra. In celebration of their love of music and their community philanthropy, Symphony subscribers Donald and Maureen Green made the lead gift of $10 million to the music center.

Maestro Bruno Ferrandis at the Santa Rosa Symphony's inaugural performance in its new home as resident orchestra of the Green Music Center.

Conductor Emeritus Corrick Brown served with SSU President Ruben Armiñana and Telecom Valley pioneer Don Green as capital campaign chairs. The Symphony worked closely with SSU's Development Office to produce numerous receptions in private homes to advance the fundraising effort. Jeffrey Kahane, who long had a goal of moving the orchestra into a space that was acoustically kind to symphonic sound, often performed at these donor gatherings.

The Santa Rosa Symphony's designation as resident orchestra is recognition well deserved for the efforts of its audience members and donors over the years who helped raise millions toward the opening of the Green Music Center. These funds included a direct donation from the Santa Rosa Symphony of $789,000 to Sonoma State University for the concert hall's acoustics. This was the largest gift from one nonprofit to another in the history of Sonoma County. The Symphony's vision of Community+Excellence became reality with a celebratory orchestral opening on the afternoon of September 30, 2012. A memorable indoor-outdoor performance featured three SRS music directors—Bruno Ferrandis and Corrick Brown conducting, and Jeffrey Kahane playing a Beethoven piano concerto. In what is the first published recording of music performed in Weill Hall, an 80-minute CD of the Santa Rosa Symphony's opening concert, *Live in Performance*, was produced in a limited souvenir edition.

Bruno Ferrandis commands the baton as he conducts the Santa Rosa Symphony in Weill Hall while Jeffrey Kahane performs a Beethoven piano concerto.

Richard Loheyde (right) and the youth orchestra have proudly performed over the years for local, regional and international audiences.

A Treasured Community Arts Organization

The Santa Rosa Symphony serves all of Sonoma County and reaches patrons to the east in Napa County and south in Marin County, drawing more than 3,000 subscribers to its classical series alone. The Symphony has expanded its program over the years, adding special choral performances, a Symphony pops concert series, youth ensembles concerts and a family concert series, which together entertain more than 55,000 audience members each year.

In addition, the Santa Rosa Symphony is recognized for having one of the most comprehensive music education programs in California. It serves nearly 20,000 students annually through its multifaceted Music for Our Schools program, four youth ensembles, a string orchestra workshop and a Summer Music Academy. The SRS Youth Orchestra, founded in 1959 as the Junior Symphony, performed at Carnegie Hall in 2002, and celebrated its 50th anniversary with a whirlwind European performance tour in the cities of Prague, Leipzig, Potsdam and Berlin in June 2009.

Joy, sorrow, tears, lamentations, laughter—to all these music gives voice, but in such a way that we are transported from the world of unrest to a world of peace, and see reality in a new way, as if we were sitting by a mountain lake and contemplating hills and woods and clouds in the tranquil and fathomless water.

— Albert Schweitzer

Beyond training musicians of the future, the Symphony has established a long-term, board-mandated educational commitment to local schools. The Free Concerts for Youth program brings thousands of schoolchildren annually to the Symphony's venue for special concerts. The SRS Education Department provides a classical music listening program—available free of charge to Sonoma County classrooms—as well as interactive in-school performances and community outreach concerts as part of a 50-plus-year commitment to preserving a musical legacy for the next generation. In September 2013, the Symphony expanded its Integrated Community Music Education family of programs to include Simply Strings, a free five-year pilot project for elementary-school children inspired by El Sistema, a publicly financed education program in Venezuela that transforms the lives of vulnerable children through music.

In July 2006, after a yearlong conductor search, French native Bruno Ferrandis was selected as the Santa Rosa Symphony's fourth music director, succeeding Jeffrey Kahane. Ferrandis impressed the search committee, board, staff and orchestra musicians with his emotional fire, dynamic technique and masterful interpretations, as well as his grace and charm. He has conducted all over the world, and his musical experience includes not only symphony and opera, but also ballet, musical theater and cinema-accompanying music.

Maestro Ferrandis was an important figure in the various preparatory events for the opening of Weill Hall. The Santa Rosa Symphony performed a concert for donors featuring pianist Berenika in February 2010—even before the concert hall chairs were installed.

Roy Zajac, principal clarinetist (center) with the Santa Rosa Symphony, also teaches music at Sonoma State University.

Left: A French horn player with the Santa Rosa Symphony helps fine-tune Weill Hall at the end of construction.

Perfecting Weill Hall's acoustics, members of the Santa Rosa Symphony played to audiences in early 2012, months before the inaugural weekend.

Ferrandis worked with musicians and acousticians in several phases of "tuning of the hall," including an event in February 2012 to which SRS subscribers and patrons were invited. The presence of hundreds of literally "warm bodies" helped technicians understand how to adjust the hall's acoustical panels for optimum sound. Symphony musicians, particularly Principal Clarinetist Roy Zajac, performed for dozens of concert hall tours and seat preview events in the years preceding Weill Hall's grand opening weekend.

In its inaugural season as resident orchestra in Weill Hall at the Green Music Center, the Santa Rosa Symphony produced more than 30 classical performances, launched the family Concert Series, hosted the Bay Area Youth Orchestra Festival, and received a first prize national ASCAP award for adventurous programming. It was a banner year of artistic vibrancy and success for both the organization and the community it serves. Both venue and orchestra are worthy of a standing ovation.

— Jennie Orvino
Marketing Associate
Santa Rosa Symphony

A Leap of Faith Pays Off in Spades

When the 1996 proposal by Don and Maureen Green to fund a choral hall at Sonoma State morphed into a vision for a world-class music venue, it was easy to get on board. The complement to the region—wine, music and tourism—seemed clear. The benefits to the University were easy to embrace.

The University's vision was bold. The board of the Santa Rosa Symphony soon signed on as an important fundraising partner, and the combination resulted in broad connections to the community. More than 1,000 new donors became engaged with the University, largely for the first time.

Good things take time. Forgotten will be the 15 years it took to complete, the fundraising challenges exacerbated by a faltering economy, and the critical leap of faith required to see it through. Critical was the leadership from the University, Symphony and major donor families.

The benefit of this project to the greater Sonoma County community will be seen over time by the positive impact that a growing, thriving University has on economic vitality and the quality of life of its region. It is enjoyable to see this future unfold.

Sam Brown
President of the Santa Rosa Symphony,
2006-2008

Chapter

9

A Glimpse Behind the Scenes

*G*reen Music Center House Manager Lori Hercs often tells her SSU student ushers that their role is similar to that of an actor in a James Bond movie. Be invisible but visible, observant but not forceful, and sophisticated and suave. She reminds them that as ushers they are part of the overall production team, and there are no small roles.

Much like an orchestra, with individual musicians contributing to performances, the behind-the-scenes GMC team synchronize their activities to professionally execute myriad subtle details to make the visitors' experience superb and memorable.

With distinctly delineated jobs, the directors of artistic administration, production, and hospitality, house manager, restaurant manager and executive chef coordinate their specific tasks months in advance. They regularly confer to choreograph all that must happen, juggling the complex needs and responsibilities of everyone ranging from internationally renowned performers to students who work as Prelude restaurant servers and concert hall ushers.

"We're a team, and I tell the student ushers this is the best team sport in which they will ever participate," said Hercs. "Every shift is a new adventure, and they have so many opportunities. This is more than just a paycheck; they're working with the community and we're the keepers of Weill Hall."

Hercs has a preshow checklist to ensure that no detail is overlooked. Her two-and-a-half-page document of tasks includes testing radios, ticket scanners, lobby chimes and intermission flashing lights. She updates ushers about specifics of each performance, late seating time and length of intermission. Hercs also makes sure signs and programs are where they are supposed to be, doors are unlocked and lights are on throughout the building.

Student workers prepare the lawn outside Weill Hall to accommodate the thousands of guests who choose to enjoy performances on the Weill Lawn on warm evenings.

"We take so much pride in this facility," she said. "This is ours and we treat it with respect. We work hard maintaining the hall's integrity, whether it's for a music class or Itzhak Perlman."

Caroline Ammann's job as director of artistic administration requires her to begin planning for each performance two years in advance. Her early knowledge of what's scheduled is crucial information for the team as its members organize their tasks to ensure a smooth concert many months later.

She interacts with the artists' agents and managers to nail down every conceivable detail, and oversees the contracts that will define what is expected for each concert. Ammann plans precise transportation and hotel arrangements, rehearsal schedules, hospitality services, facility needs and other logistics.

About three weeks prior to a

Top: Lori Hercs, Green Music Center house manager, works with student ushers prior to a performance to ensure guests have the best experience possible.

Bottom: Snoopy sits in a place of honor with student ushers ready for an event.

performance, Ammann creates a detailed production schedule, by the minute, for the GMC team to be sure that facilities will be prepped for the public, dressing rooms are set up for artists, the production crew is ready to move equipment, and security is prepared for the show. She communicates with Prelude Restaurant Managers Kindra Kautz and Josef Keller, lobby concessions staff, Box Office Manager Megan Christensen and parking staff to keep them in the loop concerning any specific needs for that day's performance. Everyone is connected by radio or cell phone.

Ammann acknowledged that it takes an extremely organized person to calmly and successfully accomplish the behind-the-scenes tasks. Rather than getting stressed out by her responsibilities, she finds her job enjoyable.

"Every artist has something they want or need on-site. The contract riders are read carefully so everything requested is given to them," said Ammann. Sometimes this means putting out a fruit tray—"no bananas"—or a tea service and water ("sparkling only please"). Every effort is made with the artists' comfort and convenience in mind. "We want them to feel comfortable here and come back. And I want to make sure all goes well."

For some artists, security is a significant issue. "It's not uncommon for an artist to have a following," said Ammann. "Sometimes that includes what we call 'pursuers.'" Before a few of the performances, she gathers members of the team to discuss any security issues, including any photos of known "pursuers" who might show up. The Green Music Center employs a private security company for indoor and outdoor crowd control and safety, and artists often come with their own. "It's critical that we are all on the same page, have the same information, and know how to handle situations."

During the concert, Ammann is typically backstage with the tour manager reviewing ticket sales and merchandise sales and doing financial reconciliation of the event.

In addition to her concert-related duties, Ammann helps organize logistics for large community fundraisers held at the GMC. When a board member or GMC donor is scheduled to attend a performance, it's Ammann's job to arrange for a meeting with an artist, if requested, and be attentive to the guest's hospitality needs.

As Director of Production Operations, Kamen Nikolov oversees the technical operations at the Green Music Center. He has a staff of five, and together they unload and supervise production gear, making sure every item is delivered to its proper place on stage and that all of the sound equipment is connected and working precisely as expected.

"I love my job. Every morning I say to myself, 'This is going to be a great day.' And it's really inspiring to meet the artists," said Nikolov, a Bulgarian native who was trained as a classical pianist and also has a background in audio recording and sound management.

Kamen Nikolov and Production Manager Jerry Uhlig have many duties, including moving pianos from the stage to a storage room after performances. Their jobs extend hours after the last guest leaves Weill Hall.

Nikolov works closely with Production Manager Jerry Uhlig and shares duties related to equipment purchases, repairs and rentals. In addition to setting up for concerts in Weill Hall, the production team oversees equipment repairs and maintenance, and handles production needs for SSU's music classrooms.

"Every day is different," said Nikolov. "Jerry and I do a lot of advance planning for a show six months out—and sometimes only one hour out. For all big events, we do fine-tuning on the day of the show to be sure we are providing everything needed on the production side." Nikolov, along with the entire production team, often works in the early morning hours after the show ends, packing up equipment trucks.

A time-consuming, though necessary, part of his job is paying all the bills related to production. This includes gear rentals, tools, supplies, piano maintenance, and fees for services and contractors.

And while all the preparations are under way, Piano Technician Larry Lobel tunes the artist's piano-of-choice (sometimes three pianos if the artist hasn't yet selected). Sonoma State has three concert Steinway pianos—two in Weill Hall, one in Schroeder Hall—and a beautiful Fazioli, signed by Herbie Hancock, which had been his touring piano.

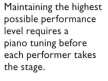

Maintaining the highest possible performance level requires a piano tuning before each performer takes the stage.

A team of workers ensure that everything is just right for not only guests, but also the performers themselves. Left to right: Caroline Ammann, director of artistic administration; Kindra Kautz, Prelude restaurant manager; Joe Gray, artist liaison; and Kelley Kaslar, hospitality director.

While the focus at the GMC is primarily on performance, hospitality services, which includes food and beverage, are an important element of the visitor experience. In addition to Prelude restaurant and concessions, hospitality includes fundraisers, catering requests, community events, wedding receptions and special college events.

Hospitality Director Kelley Kaslar was the second person hired for the GMC, and by the time Weill Hall opened she had already organized a variety of special events, including a packed schedule of summer weddings.

"I love installation days. I love the building and creation of an event before guests arrive. My idea of heaven is the day the tent arrives, and each day new vendors come in and we build the event in layers. I love constructing something out of nothing. I work with fabulous vendors and it's such a great collaboration," said Kaslar, who is a member of the Concierge Alliance of Napa Valley and Sonoma as well as the International Special Events Society.

Taking care of performers' food and beverage requests is a key part of her job, and most of the time she finds their requests to be reasonable. "No one has made us go on a major hunt," Kaslar said. "These musicians are traveling, and anything we can do to make them feel at home and more comfortable we want to do."

Kaslar described her contributions to the inaugural weekend in 2012 as "one of the most intense times of my entire life." She remembered the feeling of seeing everything in place in the gala tent as "pretty surreal . . . like having 3,500 people show up to my house. The 2012 grand opening was the most incredible experience. I get pretty excited when I see everything set up. I appreciate the little things."

She works closely with Prelude Restaurant Managers Kindra Kautz and Josef Keller, and Executive Sous-Chef Shaun Dayton.

The life of a sous-chef means preparing food not only for Prelude restaurant and outdoor diners, but also for performers and their staff and crews.

The many duties to handle include preparing the star's dressing room, vacuuming the hall, power washing the grounds, and testing sound systems.

The hospitality staff focused on developing a farm-to-table emphasis for Prelude, and have sought out Sonoma County purveyors to supply as much of the food as possible for the restaurant and special events.

Operating a restaurant that is connected to a concert hall presents unique challenges, since the dining room is open only on performance days and meals have to be timed to let patrons eat in a leisurely manner. By switching from a conventional menu to a fixed price menu, Prelude has been able to effectively accommodate diners who will be attending a performance.

SSU students are hired and trained to work as servers, prep cooks and dishwashers, and they too are sensitive to the importance of timing. It's about the overall experience.

Having clear, shiny windows and doorways adds to the elegance of Weill Hall.

Hospitality responsibilities include the dining terrace on Weill Lawn and the concessions offered in the lobby and on the lawn during performances when the back doors of the hall are open.

There are many, many others who prepare for the concert experience. The public may not know they have been there, but the custodial staff vacuum the hall, wash the windows, stock the restrooms; student workers set up tables for meals and special events throughout the building; others sort tickets, mow lawns, set the stage with risers, test the sound; and myriad other jobs not even imagined all take place at a whirlwind pace before each performance.

"Last season we had two different artists presenting over a weekend. Each had different needs and it was quite a couple of days. I think some of us got about an hour's sleep. But the artists had a very good experience, the audience loved them, and it was all worth it," said Ammann.

It does indeed take a village to pull off the exciting events and programs held at the Green Music Center. But no one's complaining—quite the opposite in fact. All are proud and pleased to be connected to this center that has already claimed international attention.

— Janet Parmer

Building a First Season,
Growing a Hall, Building a Brand

By Robert Cole

Inaugural Season Artistic Consultant

*M*y first connection with the Green Music Center was when I was still director of Cal Performances at UC Berkeley. Larry Furukawa-Schlereth, Jeff Langley and Tom Birdsall at SSU asked if they could come and talk to me about how to run a performing arts center at a university. I introduced my whole senior staff and gave the SSU group a couple hours of a workshop on how to run a performing arts center. Berkeley also had the Greek Theatre, so we had a winter season and a summer season. We had indoor and outdoor spaces. So there are a lot of similarities to the Green Music Center, but there are also some differences.

I went on and worked several years more at UC Berkeley, then retired in September 2009. The next year I was conducting a Russian orchestra around the country, conducting a ballet show in Berkeley, plus I was briefly consulting with the Napa Festival del Sol. At some point during that year, I got a call from Tom Birdsall, representing the Green Music Foundation, asking if I would be interested in talking to them further about what's going on at the Green Music Center, learning more about it.

In Fall 2010, the Green Music Foundation engaged me as a consultant, to advise in the early stages of the various issues involving this project, not knowing exactly when it was going to open at the time.

Some of the issues involved contracts for the artists. I brought contracts we could use that I had developed at Cal Performances. I also brought bylaws for a board of directors that would soon be formed. So the bylaws, the artist contracts, all of those legal kinds of documents that you need to have to function, I basically brought with me and then they were adapted to suit purposes here.

Patrons enjoy outdoor visiting with old friends— and new ones—on the Weill Lawn, outside Weill Hall.

I worked for the Green Music Foundation for six months advising and meeting with Ruben Armiñana, Marne Olson, Larry Furukawa-Schlereth, Jeff Langley and Tom Birdsall. It was all about "Well maybe this could happen and we don't know when but we're hoping maybe 2012 . . . maybe." This was now still Fall 2010, so we had time to make it happen in 2012 if we could complete the fundraising, which was unknown at the time.

So when I was in New York in January 2011 I saw Jean-Jacques Cesbron, Lang Lang's personal manager. I said, "I'm involved with this project and we're not sure if we're going to open, but if we open we would really need someone like Lang Lang. Is there any chance that he would have some dates free in September 2012?" And he said, "Well he's got one weekend date open between his American dates and his European dates." It was September 29, 2012. I asked him to hold the date until I knew if this was actually going to happen, which he did.

So we had a date, we had an artist, but we didn't know if we were going to open. So I started telling other people about the project. I went to New York and started talking about the Green Music Center—to artists, management people who manage all the biggest artists in this country and the world. They had never heard of the Green Music Center, but they had to have been thinking, "Oh yes, there's yet another place in California," because there's the symphony, the opera, there are all these operations in the Bay Area. They are all out here looking for artists too. I was just collecting information and passing it on that this great hall was going to open, although we didn't know exactly when. We hoped in September 2012, but we weren't sure *yet*.

> Music is the wine that fills the cup of silence.
>
> — Robert Fripp

In March 2011, as my time with the Green Music Foundation was ending, Larry Furukawa-Schlereth asked me if I would come on board for a year, which I did. Around this time, Sandy Weill and his wife, Joan, moved to Sonoma County, came to the center and ultimately made a generous gift. That was when we knew we were going to open in September 2012. I confirmed the date with Lang Lang's manager, and we were one step closer to the inaugural season.

Of course we wanted to have an opening that was more than just one big artist. The show deserved a broad array of talent. Jeff Langley, who was artistic director for the Green Music Center, contributed a great deal to making that work so well and beautifully. I can't think of a more perfect opening than what we had. The idea that the opening actually happened and happened so well given the fact that no one on this campus had ever done anything of that scope was really amazing—and happened so successfully.

What I did as soon as we realized we were actually going to open was to start to build an inaugural season. We were going to have to print a brochure, create a website, sell $1 million worth of tickets, etc., etc. I brought on two consultants to work with me and with the staff here: Karen Ames, publicity and public relations, because she has an international reputation and that's what we needed, and Patty Gessner, in marketing. She's had a lot of experience at the San Francisco Symphony and in the Bay Area, and knows this market very well.

I started frantically working on the season for 2012. Now that may not seem like it would be so frantic in March 2011 since you're not opening until September the next year, but if you're going to open in September 2012, you have to be selling subscriptions in April 2012. That means you have to have the season ready to go to print in January 2012 and be finished by December 2011. I had Lang Lang, but that's all I had firmed up. So Jeff Langley and I started working on the season. The Sonoma State Music Department would use the hall too, and there were a lot of little issues, details, that no one else knew except Jeff.

Ed Stolman (left) confers with Robert Cole at a reception in Prelude.

We started working, somewhat frantically, trying to find artists for 2012-13. We wanted to have a program that showcased all sides of this venue. One of the big issues is that you have 1,400 seats inside, but you also have this beautiful outdoor area, outside the back wall that opens. It had been decided that there would be tables on a terraced area for about 1,200 people and then the lawn seating behind that for another 3,000 or so. So you have a total capacity of almost 6,000 seats. We had to have an artist for the opening who would sell at least 3,000 tickets and hopefully 4,000 or 5,000. There aren't very many artists who sell that many tickets, especially when you have a venue in which acoustic music is required. You cannot get away with putting highly amplified music into that hall and expect it to work. Highly amplified music in a room that is totally made of wood is not a good idea.

Then we were looking for something in addition to classical. Jeff had the very good idea about Alison Krauss. She was coming to the Greek Theatre so I said, 'Jeff, let's go see Alison.' This was the summer of 2011. I know the guy who runs the Greek Theatre, Gregg Perloff, who used to work for Bill Graham. I told Gregg, "We're interested in Alison Krauss. We'd like to come over and see the show." It was a wonderful show and was outdoors, so it was quite grand. Theatres like the Greek do a big show, big visually, big sonically, even though she's a bluegrass artist, because it's not like a rock-and-roll band.

So we met with Gregg afterwards, and told him what we had in mind: "Could Alison come on September 30, 2012?" Now this is a big ask because people like Alison Krauss do not give you specific dates. They do a tour and if they're close to you

Robert Cole (left) welcomes SSU's Vice President Dan Condron to the black tie gala at Weill Hall's inaugural evening in 2012.

they'll do the next night, but to ask them to come so far in advance on a specific day is like asking for the moon. But we asked anyway and with the help of Gregg, we got her. We were able to confirm that Alison Krauss would come on September 30 and so had a perfect opening. Saturday night we had Lang Lang, Sunday morning we had this wonderful vocal Sunrise Concert that Jeff and his colleague Amanda McTigue put together, Sunday afternoon we had Santa Rosa Symphony's first concert there as resident orchestra, and in the evening we had Alison Krauss. Perfect.

About 6,000 people came to see Alison Krauss, but of course we had to have other artists. Most of the other artists that would be appropriate for this venue would sell between 800 and 1,400 tickets. You don't expect to sell out everything, so you shoot for 80 percent capacity. So you need artists in that neighborhood, and it was difficult because most of those artists were booked for other venues in the area or weren't available or there were other issues. I was able to get a couple of things that came directly from Carnegie Hall, major artists, but they weren't available on weekends. I only wanted a weekend series to avoid the traffic. Joyce DiDonato had to come on a Tuesday because she sang at Carnegie Hall on Saturday or Sunday and then flew out here to perform.

Of course that first year we had Yo-Yo, Lang Lang and Wynton Marsalis, who were the three big names, besides Alison Krauss, which were complete sellouts. We had others like Chucho Valdés, who did very well. We had a wonderful concert with John Adams, with the International Contemporary Ensemble from New York, which sold 1,300 tickets, which for a contemporary music program is pretty amazing. So all in all we sold about $1 million in tickets for the first year. Considering where we started that is pretty good, because we started from zero.

So then there was talk about 2013-14. From my point of view, as soon as we put 2012-13 on sale, I was worrying about 2013-14. I was panicked again with having to have artists who will sell a lot of tickets for the opening and also artists who will sell enough tickets during the rest of the year and represent the organization well. I always believe that what you're doing here in any institution like this, whether it be the opera, symphony, Cal Performances, is you're trying to build a brand. The brand is the most important thing you can have, or not have, and it says who you are and attracts certain people you need. And who do you need? You need subscribers and donors. Donors are people who will buy tickets and support a place like this, because you cannot operate a place like this unless people are willing to make contributions and not just buy tickets. If you're just selling tickets, you will not be in business. It's just not possible. In the first season we had a lot of success with that because there were some people who had already promised to support the season, which was very helpful.

Robert Cole and Jeff Langley with the oft-requested Herbie Hancock Fazioli piano, which Hancock signed with a flourish before it made its way to the Green Music Center.

So for the second season I had a little more time working with Jeff Langley again to get the top people we wanted and not just repeating what we did the year before. We ended up with a season that was quite impressive, opening with Renée Fleming, Itzhak Perlman, within the first week and Herbie Hancock to show the variety of things we do. Lang Lang came back the first week. We had to decide whether all of them would be with the back door open. Lang Lang was the only one who came on a weeknight. Weeknights scare me because of the traffic issues from other areas, but that was the only time he could come. It turned out not to be an issue because he's so big, so important an artist.

The total for the second season is 22 performances, which is two more than we did in the first season. The projected ticket sales is about $1.5 million, which is quite a bit higher than what we did the first season, for various reasons, since we have artists like Itzhak. We have one thing that is very remarkable and that is the performance by the Vienna Philharmonic Orchestra, which is a once-in-a-lifetime event. They hardly ever come to the West Coast at all and when they do, they come to Davies Hall and Disney Hall in Los Angeles and that's about it.

Our inaugural summer season was another challenge because I was under the impression, as were a number of people, that we were going to hire a director a year ago and that I shouldn't worry about the summer, somebody else is going to do that. Well then all of a sudden they didn't hire a director, and I had to worry about the summer. So again I was in panic mode because in the summer you have to sell every performance with the doors open. You have to have these major events that will sell a lot of tickets.

The slope of Schroeder Hall slides into the fading sunlight during the Green Music Center's summer concerts. Weill Hall takes advantage of Sonoma County's splendor with indoor and outdoor seating for its summer concert series.

First of all we have the opening on July 4, which was with the Santa Rosa Symphony, which is sort of a tradition around here. And then I was able to get Pink Martini, which was great and so much fun for the audience. Then we were able, with the help of Rick Bartalini, to get Josh Groban, who sold very well. He was very expensive but sold a lot of tickets, so that was fine. Then we had Chris Botti at the end of the season, who is a wonderful jazz musician with a lot of name recognition. The San Francisco Symphony did a movie music afternoon/evening. And of course one of the biggest things we had was having Yo-Yo Ma come back with what he calls his Goat Rodeo project. It is really a bluegrass kind of thing in which he brought Chris Thile and other bluegrass artists. Fabulous!

So the inaugural summer was done. We really hadn't started advertising in a big way, yet many, many tickets were sold. Information had been sent out in a brochure; we advertised in Sonoma County and had one ad in the *SF Chronicle*. We were set to open on July 4 and needed to sell thousands of tickets, which we ultimately did. I will say again, as will everyone, that a venue this large, in this location, is not going to be successful unless we can bring a broad audience from around the greater Bay Area, which we have been fairly successful in doing.

Artists express their appreciation of Weill Hall on signed photos, which line the halls backstage.

A lot of people have talked about Ruben and Marne, whose vision this was originally after they had visited Tanglewood. I studied conducting there with Lenny Bernstein some years ago. In the summer of 1970, I was a student in the conducting class and of course I've been there many times since, but you have to remember that when Koussevitzky started Tanglewood in the '30s he wasn't thinking about selling tickets to people who live in Lenox. He had this vision of it being a much larger thing than Lenox or Stockbridge, which are two small towns in the Berkshires. If you don't have that vision, forget it. That is what I've been trying to tell people—if you don't have a vision that's big enough, then you've built the wrong place. So we have to have a vision that this is going to be a place that will attract people from all over the Bay Area, and elsewhere, the whole Western United States. There are festivals at places besides Tanglewood, where people from all over the country go. This needs to be one of those places. You have to think big and you have to have vision.

So the summer 2013 was on sale and I was very optimistic about its success. I was then asked in July to put together the 2014-15 season, which meant I was already six months late. We did not yet have an opening artist, which concerned me greatly because, as I explained, it is so difficult to get a big name. You need both classical artists and more popular artists. I can manage pop artists very easily, but the classical artists are very few. The 2014-15 season and also the summer of 2014 really go hand-in-hand. The agents I was talking to are worldwide. I was dealing with people in London and so on, but the popular artists mostly have American managers. I was talking about artists, say a jazz artist, who could come for season 2014-15, but if that wasn't possible maybe he or she could come for the summer of 2014. They had to be really big names if they were going to sell a minimum of 3,000 tickets.

Weill Hall is a fantastic concert hall, but it is limiting also. There are a lot of things you cannot do there. You cannot do plays or big dance shows because of the nature of the building. It is a concert hall. You cannot do a rock-and-roll show or very high decibel shows like you can do at the Greek Theatre, where it's totally open space.

Also of course there's Schroeder, the smaller recital hall, which would open in 2014-15. I'm quite prepared to plan for that as well. It is very small, and there are many artists for smaller venues who will do very well there and contribute to the artistic and educational part of this whole project.

The other thing I found very important was staying in touch with the faculty and the academic mission. That was probably the most important goal during my tenure at Berkeley. Whatever success I had was dependent on that aspect. When I got there, there was no board of directors so we created one, and it was very effective. Also there was not much organized fundraising going on. Establishing the board and creating this close relationship with the faculty and the academic side were the two keys to bringing in so many great artists. To make it really successful, and that is what needs to happen here, there has to be an educational component. That takes time. It's not something you can accomplish in two or three years, but it should be the goal. I'm pleased to note that great strides in this area are already occurring.

So for me it has been a real pleasure working with Sonoma State; I have enjoyed it. There have been many difficult things to manage, partially because of the uncertainty as we've gone along. This is really a start-up, and fortunately I've done more than one start-up in my life. I have to say what I've enjoyed a lot is working with the staff here. I don't think there was one person here who had ever done this before, running a performing arts center. So I have Caroline Ammann with whom I'm working, and she's learned all these things so quickly and is so competent. I have also enjoyed working with Ryan Ernst, our marketing guy; he's very savvy at marketing but he'd never done this before, the performing arts side of it, and it is a totally different world than selling whatever it was he was selling before. It's been really great to have the opportunity to work with these young people, and I've enjoyed it even with all the bumps in the road that we have experienced and survived.

I think everyone should be proud and amazed that we've had the success we have had, because this place is now on the map and not just in Northern California, but nationwide and worldwide. So now artists and artists' agents know about the Green Music Center and Weill Hall, and they're saying to us, "We have so and so. They are playing Carnegie Hall, playing Kennedy Center, can they come to the Green Music Center?" This is big stuff; this is what's happened in not even two years. A lot of things have happened. My three years were a part-time job on overdrive!

City on a Hill

Ruben Armiñana and his charming wife, Marne Olson, had a vision. They visited the Tanglewood Music Center in western Massachusetts and envisioned how a similar facility could be created on the campus of Sonoma State University. With determination, vision, humor and steadfastness, they saw the project become a reality. As a result of their tireless efforts and ability to overcome countless challenges, the Green Music Center with its jewel box Weill Hall is, indeed, a City on a Hill where world-class music is performed in an acoustically superb facility. As one who formerly chaired the Board of Trustees of the California State University system, I both thank you and salute you for your vision and tenacity—and for making the Green Music Center a destination location.

Larry Gould
California State University Board of Trustees
1996-2002

Experiencing the Possibilities
of "Educate All"

A Living, Breathing Classroom Fulfills a Vision

Long before the dream of the Green Music Center, Weill Hall and Schroeder Hall was realized, the intention was to build a world-class music center that was fully integrated with the academic mission of Sonoma State University. The phrase "Aim high. Reach wide. Educate all." was adopted to underscore the vision for a facility that would blend world-class performances with educational opportunities for people of all ages and backgrounds.

Sonoma State is a residential public liberal arts and sciences university committed to giving its students a broad-based education, regardless of their chosen discipline. Striving to ensure that graduates have the competencies valued by employers or graduate programs is important to the campus. Students leave SSU with discipline-specific knowledge and the ability to think critically, innovate, communicate, work in teams and solve problems.

The GMC is instrumental in strengthening SSU's commitment to liberal arts education. Sonoma State is unique among public schools in the nation, and increasingly students are choosing SSU because of the GMC and the strong academic links we are developing. In just the first year of performances at Weill Hall, students have had the opportunity to attend concerts by celebrated artists such as cellist Yo-Yo Ma and pianist Lang Lang and many other famed and talented performers.

With the second performance season, student opportunities for attending concerts increased due to the "rush" ticket program offering last-minute tickets at a much-reduced cost. The campus is largely residential, and co-curricular events are important for providing learning opportunities for students beyond the classroom.

Giving youths the opportunity to perform on the stage at Weill Hall before an audience of friends and families is an experience they will treasure.

While it is hard to predict the range of academic interactions that will evolve in the years ahead, it is clear that these will be varied and interdisciplinary and will serve to radiate creativity across the campus. Such transforming experiences will ensure that students at SSU explore their present while creating their future. The promise of the Green Music Center will ensure that SSU is a preferred destination campus in the years ahead. At a recent orientation new students were asked who had traveled the farthest. An incoming student from Connecticut won and when asked why, she answered simply, "Because of the Green Music Center."

As we always imagined, the Green Music Center is much more than a performance venue—it is a living, breathing classroom.

— Andrew Rogerson
Vice President for Academic Affairs
Chief Academic Officer

Academic Integration: More Than Just a Pretty Place

What happens when you mix a world-class music hall with a university campus? A little bit of everything.

When a professor of physics looks at Weill Hall, he sees a place for students to analyze the dynamics of sound. A business professor pushes his students to develop entrepreneurial thinking by inventing new ways to use a performance hall. A dance professor challenges her students to choreograph routines built on sounds collected at the nearby nature preserve.

On nearly 100 days of the year, the Green Music Center opens its doors to the public for performances of the highest caliber. From symphonies and vocalists to jazz and world music, the stage of Weill Hall plays host to some of the world's brightest musical stars. But that's only a part-time role. On the other 265 days of the year, the GMC is a vital part of the Sonoma State University fabric. Weill Hall and Schroeder Hall can transform into a lecture space, a laboratory, a workshop and a classroom.

With this year-round functionality in mind, the GMC Board of Advisors and SSU President Ruben Armiñana allocated nearly $200,000 over two years to support interdisciplinary programs that unite the University campus with the GMC. "These projects encourage both faculty and students to look for novel and creative ways to integrate the arts with other disciplines in the University," said Marne Olson, vice-chair of the GMC Board of Advisors. "The ability to 'think outside the box' is crucial." The Green Music Center Board of Advisors' University Affairs Committee, comprised of faculty, students, staff and administration, reviews and selects academic integration projects annually.

These first examples of the Academic Integration Project lay the groundwork for future creative collaborations between the campus community and the many venues of the Green Music Center.

Using Weill Hall as a teaching and learning platform allows students to get out of the classroom and have experiential learning opportunities.

Proposals funded include:

CREATIVE ARTS AND DIGITAL MEDIA ENTREPRENEURSHIP, *Business*

> Students in this certificate course learned firsthand how to launch, grow and harvest their own business endeavors.

MUSIC, THE DIGITAL WAY, *Engineering*

> Hands-on activities in Weill Hall to enhance students' understanding of digital signal processing through music and concert hall acoustics.

SOUND STUDIO UPGRADE & REDNET, *Music*

> Teaching recording skills to students in support of live concert recordings in the newly renovated sound engineering studio in Ives Hall.

SOUNDSCAPE PROJECT, *SSU Preserves*

> Engaging biology, engineering and performing arts students to create original recordings and dance inspired by natural soundscapes.

Expanding the use of Weill Hall and the Green Music Center to include academic projects of all disciplines brings new opportunities for learning.

OAKLAND SCHOOL FOR THE ARTS COLLABORATION, *Theatre Arts & Dance*

A partnership with the Oakland School for the Arts, a K-12 magnet school devoted to intensive pre-professional training in the arts.

STEM SYMPOSIUM, *Mathematics*

A convention that highlights the University's commitment to STEM education— science, technology, engineering and mathematics.

AN EXPOSURE TO CHEMISTRY, *Chemistry*

A lecture by Nobel Laureate Dr. Lou Ignarro and an exploration of wine chemistry by Dr. Phil Crews of UC Santa Cruz.

FRESHMAN COMMON READ, *Writing Center, Associated Student Productions, Transition Programs*

A campus-wide initiative to integrate common reading curriculum and master classes for first-time freshmen.

ARTS & HUMANITIES SOPHOMORE SYMPOSIUM, *Modern Languages & Literatures, Communications Studies, Arts & Humanities*

Weekly lectures in Schroeder Hall and a culminating symposium throughout Weill Hall and Lawn.

PERFORMANCE ART AND SOCIAL JUSTICE, *Arts & Humanities*

Cutting-edge performance art highlighting how social issues affect individuals and communities.

SSU WORKS, *Theatre Arts & Dance, SSU Preserves*

Increasing public awareness of sustainability issues through events, performances and programs.

PEDAGOGICAL SUPPORT OF PHYSICS & COMPUTER SCIENCES, *Physics, Engineering, Computer Science*

Using the Green Music Center as a laboratory to explore principles of music, audio and acoustics.

PRECISION MEASUREMENTS OF CONCERT HALL & CLASSROOM ACOUSTICS, *Physics & Astronomy*

Observing the acoustic parameters of music and speech to demonstrate the effectiveness of acoustical elements throughout the Green Music Center.

First-of-Its-Kind Residencies

Weill Hall Artists-in-Residence — Trio Ariadne

Given the Green Music Center's long-standing educational commitments and Sandy Weill's history at the helm of Carnegie Hall, a relationship with this esteemed arts organization was destined to occur. Professors and administrators from Sonoma State University were introduced to Sir Clive Gillinson, executive and artistic director of Carnegie Hall, and Sarah Johnson, director of Carnegie Hall's Weill Music Institute. Together, the group crafted an innovative residency program to unite the East and West Coast worlds of education, outreach and performance. The first-of-its-kind program was launched in 2013, introducing SSU students to graduates of The Academy, a prestigious program of Carnegie Hall, The Juilliard School and the Weill Music Institute in collaboration with the New York City Department of Education.

Instructing, performing for and living among SSU students, the chamber music group Trio Ariadne—all Weill Hall Artists-in-Residence—joined the campus community to serve as mentors for music

The first-ever artists-in-residence, Trio Ariadne, delighted audiences and created learning experiences through their work within the residential community, on campus and in the local community.

students and offer workshops on topics such as practical internships and career pathways. This innovative collaboration by Elizabeth Joy Roe, Carol McGonnell and Sæunn Thorsteinsdottir fused instruction, outreach, residency and performance, intimately exposing SSU students to some of the nation's finest postgraduate musicians.

They provided instruction and service for the Music Department and its students through chamber music and solo coaching, studio lessons for individual players, and serving as visiting artists in music department classes.

As part of their residency, the Trio offered programs and services enhancing the educational mission of the University. They contributed to the stature of performing arts in the community through concert series for the campus and local K-12 schools. In addition, the Trio performed in Weill Hall.

This residency provided a link between three campus units: the Department of Music, the Office of Residential Life and the Green Music Center.

Alvin Ailey Dance Legacy Residency

As the two sides of Sandy Weill's musical world were coming together, Joan Weill's influence at Alvin Ailey American Dance Theater was also spreading to the SSU campus. As a board member at Alvin Ailey since 1994—and chairwoman from 2000 to 2014—

Joan has been acknowledged as a driving force in the growth of the entire Ailey organization over the past two decades. Most notable among her many accomplishments is the creation of Ailey's purpose-built permanent home—named The Joan Weill Center for Dance in her honor—New York's largest building dedicated to dance, which opened in 2005. Mrs. Weill has demonstrated an equal commitment to both the company's artistry as well as Ailey's Arts-In-Education programs, which reach 100,000 young people annually across the country.

The Ailey Legacy College Residency at Sonoma State University began in the early weeks of 2013, consisting of dance classes and public lectures by founding Ailey II Artistic Director Sylvia Waters (1974-2012). The residency brought a direct experience of Ailey to the students, highlighting him as one of America's foremost dance artists and an advocate for African-American cultural experiences.

Joan Weill, a longtime fan and former chair of the Alvin Ailey American Dance Theater, is an active supporter of the group, sharing her vast experience in the arts.

Engaging K-12 Communities

Picture a sixth-grade musician from a local school standing on the stage of Weill Hall, looking out at family and friends who have come to hear her perform. Will she imagine herself capable of so much more now that she has been encouraged to step into that inspiring space?

That is the hope of the K-12 outreach program, said Dan Condron, vice president for university affairs and coordinator of the K-12 effort. Young people will dare to see themselves differently. At the same time, they will be exposed to the world of higher education.

Sonoma State University has long had many connections to the K-12 schools of its six-county region, exposing young students to the world of higher education in order to open doors to their future. Most University departments on campus maintain long-running programs that have shown young people the various avenues to success that a college degree can provide.

Many groups of schoolchildren have experienced performing in Weill Hall through efforts to connect K-12 with the Green Music Center and the University.

The Green Music Center made its first official connection to the K-12 community in 2013 with two unique performances in Weill Hall by local students.

Nine Waldorf schools from Sonoma and Marin Counties took to the Weill Hall stage to perform a unique musical piece before more than 1,000 of their classmates, parents and the public. "How great it was for our students to taste what it is like to be on a high-end professional stage! The inspiration can inform the rest of their lives," said Chip Romer, director of Credo High School in Rohnert Park, who produced the event.

It was also important for the families who attended, Romer observed. "Imagine going to a place outside your family's normal cultural practice and the pride of seeing your son or daughter on stage in Weill Hall. 'Waldorf at Weill' introduced so many new people to the opportunities at the Green Music Center."

On the same evening, Waldorf students and families also had the opportunity to engage with members of University admissions staff and representatives from various academic departments. In this way, they gained an exciting look at higher education in their community.

Just one week later, students from the Santa Rosa City School District made their way to Weill Hall for the William Barclay Memorial Scholarship Concert, featuring choirs from all the district's high schools. This annual event serves as a fundraiser for choral student scholarships. It featured more than 200 students in a two-hour performance, with Sonoma State University's Jenny Bent, director of choral activities, serving as guest conductor for the evening.

"Hosting the students, parents and educators from our community for performances such as these is an honor for Sonoma State University, and is the first of many examples of how the Green Music Center will bridge K-12 education with higher learning," said Condron. More K-12 performances are planned in the future.

— Jean Wasp

"Aim high. Reach wide." I am proud to have written that. Or let me rephrase: I am honored to have had those values come through me onto the blank page way back in 2002 as I huddled with the conceivers of the Green Music Center. What fun to think big with big thinkers. What fun to thread language through giant ideas, gradually rendering the unimaginable into the sharply imagined. From there, it was but a hop, skip and a jump (translate: years of deep, life-swallowing personal persistence by so many heroic people) to the miracle of the real.

The vision of the Green Music Center kills me. It always has. It still does. A hub of inspiration. A campus that is, itself, a multidimensional analog of excellence. A center that weaves together artifice, edifice and nature.

This is a location that relocates our preconceptions, for we're not inside some European palace, squeezed into an East Coast bastion of sometimes glorious, sometimes restrictive tradition. No, we are out on the left coast—in literal left field—situated between strawberry patches and acres of alfalfa, just up the road from the organic meat guy on one side and the organic vegetable guy on the other.

It's a part of the world where formal is loose, playful, young. It's a part of the world tuned to the sky, the air, the sun. It's a part of the world that says, "Why not?" to imagination.

(Editor's Note: Philanthropist and SSU friend Ed Stolman later suggested adding the words "Educate all," which completed the overarching concept for the Green Music Center of "Aim high. Reach wide. Educate all.")

Amanda McTigue
Artistic Consultant

Parts of the Creative Mix

*T*he Green Music Center has provided a place for a wide range of audiences and students to experience the possibilities within themselves in new ways. The heart and soul of the project is education. Educate All has been the mantra for the facility since its creation. What has been possible, thanks to the extraordinary spaces within the Center, has already touched many lives, young and old.

The goal is to create a national model for how a symphony orchestra, a university and a community can work together to engage one another—and together become the best that they can be. Some of the programs to facilitate music education and performance are:

SSU's Music Department – Everyone Performs

Since its national accreditation in 1972, the SSU Music Department has had a prime edict: everyone performs. A commitment to active involvement stands at the heart of the music curriculum.

"We value music of different cultures, ethnic groups, formal styles and historical periods," said Music Chair Brian Wilson. It shows in the wide range of opportunities offered to all majors, who gain experience with both the intuitive and the intellectual processes of the art.

The department made its home within the Green Music Center in 2008 and uses Schroeder Hall as an expanded classroom for instruction and performance. Music students and faculty also have use of Weill Hall as a living laboratory, to hone their instrumental and vocal skills in a facility built for world-class performances.

Table seating fills the tiered lawn for the Green Music Center's summer concert series, with sloped lawn seating for picnickers at the rear.

From faculty and guest artist recitals to large and small student ensembles, the department presents more than 100 performances every year, reaching 9,000+ audience members. Most are low cost or free.

Following their public performances, some of the amazing array of artists who appeared at Weill Hall have allowed students to learn from them, including Barbara Cook, Wynton Marsalis, The Silk Road Ensemble and the San Francisco Symphony.

As a fully invested partner in music education, the Music Department hosts numerous high-school music festivals each year, and faculty members are in demand as conductors, clinicians and performers. The Music Department is also a cultural resource for the campus and the community, through both its busy roster of student performances and the professional activities of its faculty.

Top: Sonoma State music professor Cliff Hugo speaks to the SSU jazz ensemble in one of the student rehearsal spaces of Music Education Hall.

Bottom: Weill Hall is a living laboratory for music students, as SSU choral director Jenny Bent leads an SSU singing ensemble in a rehearsal.

SSU's OCP (On Campus Presents)

OCP, a student-centered programming group, features entertainment ranging from contemporary and Top 40 artists to the nation's most requested comedy acts. Taking place in Weill Hall and at other campus venues, OCP performances attract a range of patrons, from students, faculty and staff to families in local communities. Highly acclaimed speakers and lecturers bridge the gap between academics and entertainment, making OCP a true co-curricular endeavor.

MasterCard Performance Series

The fast finish to the main concert hall and grounds at the Green Music Center seemed priceless enough, then MasterCard entered the picture in July 2012, thanks to Joan and Sandy Weill's introduction. In the first corporate partnership of its kind for the University, MasterCard and SSU cemented a long-term relationship in support of the performing arts. This led to the annual MasterCard Performance Series—never before seen in the region.

MasterCard forged a first-of-its-kind partnership with the University, leading to the popular MasterCard Performance Series.

I have been fortunate to have performed in many of the great concert halls around the world. After playing in the Green Music Center, it is my belief that the sound in the hall is the equal of venues such as Orchestra Hall in Boston, the KKL hall in Lucerne, Switzerland, and even the Musikverein in Vienna. It has sonic qualities which are essential to a performer for optimum musical expression. Beautiful, soft dynamics and the ability to handle loud dynamics without any harshness or distortion whatsoever. The Green Music Center also offers the listener a connection to the performance which will only enhance the experience.

— John Engelkes
Trombone, San Francisco Symphony

San Francisco Symphony

The sweet strings of the San Francisco Symphony filled Weill Hall for its first three seasons, drawing crowds to experience the new hall's beautiful sound.

A significant relationship with the San Francisco Symphony was announced in early 2012, when the Grammy Award-winning orchestra signed a multi-year concert agreement to perform at the Green Music Center. The symphony headed north to help inaugurate the brand-new Green Music Center on the SSU campus in 2012. Four Thursday evening concerts of exceptional artistry were offered. From a new commission to audience favorites and wildly popular guest artists, the series had something for everyone. "We are eager to welcome audiences to this stunning new venue and share the inspired music-making that is the trademark of the vibrant partnership between the San Francisco Symphony and Michael Tilson Thomas," said the symphony's Executive Director Brent Assink.

— Jean Wasp

Resident Conductor Donato Cabrera and the San Francisco Symphony rise before a performance at Weill Hall.

13

Inaugural Weekends:
Galas Full of Good Omens

The Green Music Center inaugural weekend was blessed with good omens, as a harvest moon shone over Weill Hall on Saturday and a brilliant sunrise maneuver awed the audience with its timing on Sunday morning.

World-renowned pianist Lang Lang performed to a wildly enthusiastic crowd on Saturday evening and welcomed guests to "this great new hall." Even Lang Lang knew it had been a long, long time in coming. But it was worth the wait. Afterward, the Chinese superstar confessed that he had performed seven works—three Mozart piano sonatas and four Chopin ballades—for the first time that night. "So let's do something new each time," he said, sounding a note for the future.

The hundreds of guests who walked the red carpet installed on the Koret Grand Entry—a gift of the Koret Foundation—toward the reception and performance area brought a touch of elegance to the evening with their ball gowns and tuxedos. The air was alive with excitement.

Thousands dressed warmly to brave the 50-degree weather to sit outside on Weill Lawn. They were rewarded with an intimate and mesmerizing look at the concert on jumbo monitors that displayed Lang Lang from multiple camera angles, including one from a camera mounted inside the Steinway piano.

Lang Lang played two encores, responding to demands from the audience both inside and out. One guest thought the hall's acoustics seemed "brighter" with the doors open, which occurred for the first time that evening.

Lang Lang receives a standing ovation after his performance on inaugural weekend 2012.

Honored guests at the 2012 inaugural weekend included Governor Jerry Brown and his wife, Anne Gust Brown, who joined Joan and Sanford Weill at the gala event.

SSU's resident piano legend Marilyn Thompson observed how Lang Lang's idiosyncratic playing thrilled the audience. "Lang Lang found and used so many of the truly unique qualities of the American Steinway piano he played to portray the musical dialogue and character of each piece that he performed," she said. "It was as though he and the piano were having a profound conversation with one another. And not one sound—from the very hushed pianissimo to the most tumultuous fortissimo—was lost in the phenomenal acoustics of Weill Hall."

The celebratory mood throughout the evening excited longtime supporters as well as the new friends who were a part of the gala event. "Weill Hall is a jewel, both in sound and physical beauty. We are fortunate to have it in our backyard. The University and the Sonoma County community have an enduring world-class cultural center that will attract national and international performers in the years to come," said Joseph Pogar Jr., a patron who, with his wife, attended their very first symphony concert in 2012.

The Wine Country elite from both Sonoma and Napa Counties and San Francisco rubbed shoulders with Governor Jerry Brown and First Lady Anne Gust Brown, Congresswoman Nancy Pelosi and her husband, Paul, Congresswoman Lynn Woolsey, MasterCard CEO Ajay Banga and his wife, Ritu, many Bank of America officials, and local legislators at an event that was only imagined a year before, when planning began.

"Sonoma State University is the kind of place where good things happen at the last minute," said President Ruben Armiñana in his opening remarks, noting the early history of the University, which had been created by the stroke of a pen with last-minute legislation in 1960.

Opening the gala dinner, President Ruben Armiñana expressed his pleasure to be at inaugural weekend after many years of planning and work.

The evening was full of speeches and tributes to founders Donald and Maureen Green, Santa Rosa Symphony Conductor Emeritus Corrick Brown, Conductor Laureate Jeffrey Kahane, Joan and Sandy Weill, and the 1,800 donors who contributed $72 million as the project grew from a vision of a small choral space in the 1990s to the $128 million facility it is today. Armiñana paid particular homage to his wife, Marne, who he said was primarily responsible for the Green Music Center's role in the cultivation of the arts at a state university. "Not only does Marne have great vision, but she's got tenacity, which came in very handy on this project," he said.

Thousands of guests attended the inaugural weekend events, some of whom chose to sit outside; others preferred to be inside Weill Hall. The excitement of the evening was seen and felt everywhere, capped by a spectacular fireworks display.

Joan and Sandy Weill, new Sonoma County residents whose $12 million donation boosted the project to completion in 2012, lauded their friend Lang Lang, whom they first met when the pianist was 17. "I told him then he was the Tiger Woods of the piano," Sandy Weill joked. "But now I think we are going to have to change that." Lang Lang, who has been supported by the Weills in his efforts to create his own music foundation for young artists, called the couple "my favorite people in the world."

Rohnert Park Council Member Gina Belforte said the facility is not only a stage for world-class performers but will offer inspiration to future students who will choose to come to Sonoma State to study and pursue their passion for music. This idea was spelled out many times throughout the evening by those who commented on the new cultural opportunities that will be possible for the region.

A musical fireworks display followed Lang Lang's performance before guests made their way to the elegant white tent behind Prelude for a special dinner featuring a menu by celebrity chef Michael Chiarello. Guests were treated to music by the University Jazz Band before the dinner and were serenaded afterward as they left past midnight. Observers said that nearly a third of those at the reception appeared to be new to the campus, confirming what many said, that this music center will help make new friends for the University.

SSU communications professor Ed Beebout asked Democratic leader Nancy Pelosi about her impression of the event. "Tonight we saw a real tribute to the people of Sonoma County. The vision, the building, the appreciation of an other-worldly performance like Lang Lang's was awe-inspiring. We saw the generosity and graciousness of the Greens and the Weills, and we heard some fabulous music," she said.

MasterCard CEO Ajay Banga told Beebout that his sponsorship of the opening season is part of what his company can do very well: to offer their customers a "priceless" experience. "What can be more priceless than the kind of location that this University and this hall provides? The location of a school like Sonoma State University and a hall like this is an outstanding vision, and we want to be a part of it," he said.

Armiñana said at the dinner that those who had been known in the early days of the project as "the Three Accents"—himself (Cuban), Corrick Brown (American) and Donald Green (English)—and had made hundreds of appearances throughout the community in the initial years of fundraising, would now be joined by a new accent— a New York one—with the involvement of Joan and Sandy Weill.

At the dinner, Donald Green spoke movingly about his and his wife Maureen's initial vision for a choral space as a way to create a rich cultural center in Sonoma County that would attract engineers and others to the then-burgeoning Telecom Valley industry that he was pioneering at the time.

Donald and Maureen Green (seated) received thankful applause from those who attended the gala dinner at the 2012 inaugural weekend.

Many shared Armiñana's sentiment that what happened that Saturday night was only a hint of what is to come. Noted Sonoma County historian and columnist Gaye LeBaron said at the reception that the outcome of the project fits in with her "third law of progress: everything always takes 20 years."

— Jean Wasp

Santa Rosa Symphony – Home at Last

After six years with Bruno Ferrandis as music director and more than 15 years of developing the vision of a new performance home in a world-class venue, the Santa Rosa Symphony celebrated its 85th birthday with a roaring twenties-themed gala on October 5, 2012. The "Roaring Celebration" occupied not only the concert hall but also the magnificent lobby at ground floor and choral circle levels. The evening honored Sonoma County cultural icons Donald Green and Corrick Brown and included poignant tributes to both.

The celebration also capped a week of Weill Hall inaugural season activities, which garnered a wealth of media attention. Santa Rosa Symphony's opening concert, on the blazing hot afternoon of September 30, 2012, was mentioned and reviewed in more than 20 regional and national publications, including the *New York Times*, *San Francisco Chronicle* and *Symphony* magazine.

KRON television's *Bay Area Backroads* aired a feature, and National Public Radio broadcast a portion of the orchestral opening performance. A highlight of the musical program was *Sonoma Overture*, a world premiere by prominent composer Nolan Gasser, commissioned by Santa Rosa Symphony for this grand occasion. Also performed were Beethoven's *Consecration of the House*, conducted by Corrick Brown; and Beethoven's *Piano Concerto No. 4*, Copland's *Canticle of Freedom*, featuring a 100-person choir; and audience favorite Ravel's *Bolero*, all conducted by Bruno Ferrandis.

Audiences experienced the first performance in the fully open Weill Hall of the Santa Rosa Symphony as resident orchestra. The house was full and the lawn was brimming with guests as a new dawn began for Sonoma State University.

In addition to the audience inside, this concert was notable for the 3,000 guests occupying the Weill Lawn, either at tables covered with elaborate picnics and wine, or sprawled on blankets on the grass under the shade of trees or multicolored umbrellas. As the music was amplified and large video screens provided some up-close views of the orchestra, the joy and excitement outdoors was palpable. Young children frolicked on the hillside with no need to be shushed by their parents.

> — Jennie Orvino
> Marketing Associate
> Santa Rosa Symphony

Sunrise Choral Concert – A New Dawn Awaits

Some of them drove through mist-bound Sonoma roads to get there, but the 1,200 people who arrived at Weill Hall on a very early Sunday morning were not disappointed. As part of the inaugural weekend of the Green Music Center and Weill Hall's opening, an inspirational sunrise choral concert reached for the heavens in the staging of an intimate consecration of the hall, symbolizing the many voices to come.

And the heavens cooperated.

On stage for a 45-minute performance were 200 singers from various community choruses conducted by Sonoma State Choral Director Jenny Bent. They included the SSU Symphonic Chorus, Maria Carrillo High School Chamber Singers, Santa Rosa Children's Chorus and Cantiamo Sonoma. Soloists were local legends and Music Department alumni Carol Menke and Christopher Fritzsche, with Jenni Samuelson.

SSU Professor and Director of Opera and Musical Theatre Lynne Morrow introduced the morning program, describing the hall as "a vessel that will transport us to new worlds, to have transcendent experiences." She continued, "This hall will create community," and it is about "making a joyful noise."

Morrow invited the audience to participate in the final chorus, called "Every Little Minute"—music composed by Jeff Langley and text by librettist Amanda McTigue—with the rest of the singers. She ended with words by Jelaluddin Rumi, the 13th-century mystic poet.

As Christopher Fritzsche sang the line "It's the angle of the light," the sun's rays broke through the mist as if on cue, and the hall was bathed in golden light. Many were brought to tears as the idea of a new dawn for the future of the arts in the community became more apparent with every note.

The audience was filled with friends and families of the chorus members, long-time community supporters and well-known donors. SSU President Ruben Armiñana and his wife, Marne Olson, and philanthropists Joan and Sandy Weill attended. Green Music Center founders Donald and Maureen Green, and their daughter Rebecca and son-in-law Tom Birdsall and their family, were acknowledged by a standing ovation at the concert's close.

A practiced and impressive children's choir was led by Professor Jenny Bent at the Sunrise Concert on inaugural weekend.

Composer and GMC Artistic Director Jeff Langley played the piano as Jenny Bent led the choruses in Langley's original work entitled "Dedicated to You," with text composed by McTigue. They were swarmed by well-wishers at the end of the concert.

As soprano soloist Menke left the hall, she beamed, "You can sing anything in that hall and sound like a million bucks."

Langley has spoken passionately about the mission of using the Green Music Center as a focus for building community and remembering the reasons why the Center was built: to inspire and cherish artistic expression in its many forms. He and McTigue had been sensitive to dedicating each segment of the performance to the many supporters who made the long journey to this day.

As she stood in the warm light of the morning in the eastern side of the hall, Marne Olson could hardly contain her enthusiasm for what was to come. "We're looking toward the future and there is so much we can do now . . . more music, more art, spoken word, poetry. We can continue to get the students and faculty involved. This is going to be a place for all ages."

— Jean Wasp

Alison Krauss Concert: A Personal Account

by C. E. McAuley

Communication Studies Faculty

September 2012

Called "the voice of American music," Alison Krauss and her band, Union Station, took to the stage in Weill Hall at the Green Music Center—a culmination of the weekend of opening ceremonies for the new musical heart of the North Bay.

Gone were Governor Jerry Brown and the black tie celebrations from the evening before. It was "Community Day" and it showed. This was the night when Weill Hall, quite literally, opened itself up to the public—a public that was more than 6,000 strong and ready to celebrate.

"I've never seen anything like this," said Krauss. "We're honored to be here." For Krauss and her band, it was the last stop on a two-year world tour. For the audience at Weill Hall, it was the beginning of a musical journey that will last generations. And the people knew it.

When I arrived on the red carpet with my parents, both folk singer-songwriters and members of the Grammys who have walked that other red carpet, the mellow, happy Sonoma County vibe was definitely present. But there was also something else: excitement.

People were more than happy to be there; they felt a sense of pride. It was obvious listening to passing conversation that the feeling of being a part of something, well, magical, was shared by the members of the audience. My parents certainly felt it as well. So did I.

President Ruben Armiñana talked to the audience before the show and said he had heard that "this was the most exciting event to happen since 1937," alluding to the celebration of the construction of the Golden Gate Bridge.

As I showed my parents the grounds of the Green Music Center before the concert, it was obvious that despite the more than decade-long struggle to complete the project, it had been realized in a major way. The organization for this culminating event of the opening weekend was truly astounding.

My concerns about parking, for instance, proved to be unfounded. I had detailed conversations before the show about my parking strategy to make certain that quick post-concert getaway was possible. It turned out the folks at SSU Police and Parking Services already thought about that, and after an enjoyable and historic evening we just rolled away into the Sonoma County night.

Even the staffers and many students seemed very excited to be working at the event. At the box office was a student from my media law class, which I teach in one of the Green Music Center (Music Education Hall) classrooms, beaming and helping patrons left and right. The students were identified by name and major on the box office window—a good conversation starter for those new to musical events on a college campus. There were student ticket scanners, student ushers and more. Everyone was enthusiastic and well informed on topics ranging from the concert to even the type of wood used to build the floor and chairs in Weill Hall.

And, yes, I enjoyed the concert greatly. But what I really kept thinking about the entire time was what it would be like 50 years from now to look back on all the luminaries that will eventually take to this stage and how I was there with my family at the very beginning.

Alison Krauss and Union Station were a hit with audiences as they performed their bluegrass/country music for a full house and packed lawn.

A Wonderful Thing We Have Created

Speech given by Donald Green at September 29, 2012, Inaugural Season Gala Dinner

What a wonderful thing we have created. All of us from Sonoma County and the North Bay should feel very proud.

For me this project started almost 15 years ago. I was having lunch with Bob Worth. He was a professor and the director of choral music at Sonoma State University, and Maureen and I were members of his community choir. During lunch we agreed that it was a pity that SSU did not have a suitable venue on campus to perform choral music. Without a great deal of thought, I said that one of the companies I had founded was going public in a few weeks and, if it was successful, Maureen and I would contribute to a fund to build an on-campus choral hall.

A short time later, and after my company went public, Dr. and Mrs. Armiñana invited us to dinner to discuss and refine our choral hall proposal. As it happened, Ruben already had a clear idea of what he wanted, and that was a replica of Ozawa Hall at Tanglewood in Massachusetts, the summer home of the Boston Symphony Orchestra. He had been there and fallen in love with it. We concluded our dinner with Maureen and I making a donation of $5 million and also committing to visit Tanglewood.

Tanglewood lived up to its reputation; the acoustics were superb, the ambiance was pleasant and elegant. The impact of Tanglewood on the local community was also very positive. Hotels and restaurants were plentiful and flourishing. Other performing arts venues and cultural activities, including dance, theater and museums, were thriving, and the sound of music was all around. The cost of constructing the concert hall was relatively modest at about $10 million. We were so impressed that we committed an additional $5 million in a matching grant toward the construction of a similar venue in Sonoma.

We came home from Tanglewood energized. Architects were chosen; the site was selected. We partnered with the Santa Rosa Symphony, which is now the resident orchestra, and fundraising began in earnest.

Ruben Armiñana, Corrick Brown and I became known as the three accents—Cuban, American and English. We were welcomed into many homes to communicate the project's vision and to raise funds. We lost track of how many presentations we made—probably more than 100. Many friendships were formed, many commitments were made, and more than 1,600 donors responded. The capital campaign became the largest ever in Sonoma and Napa Wine Country. For nine summers, we also enjoyed a festival known as the Green Music Festival that demonstrated the type of musical, arts and educational programming that could be featured at the Green Music Center.

While we were fundraising, the outside world did not stay constant. Changes were made to the overall concept. We had what the military called mission creep. In our case it was more like mission gallop. The cost of materials rose dramatically due to a construction boom in China, and we rode the dot-com bubble up and down. With all of this financial turmoil, I am reminded of this quote, partially by Rudyard Kipling: "If you can keep your head when all about you are losing theirs, you probably don't know what's going on." I personally would like to thank Ruben and SSU for maintaining their commitment to building a world-class, acoustically marvelous concert hall with uncompromising standards.

So here we are today. Why did we support this project and work on it for more than 15 years? Well, from the beginning I have cited three reasons:

- First, as a choral singer it is important to hear clearly the voices surrounding you to blend and harmonize to get maximum pleasure from the performance for both the performers and the audiences. The acoustical perfection that our new Weill Hall has achieved will enable musical magic to take place.

- Second, as an entrepreneur and employer, and having founded three companies and seed-funded many more in the North Bay, I have always needed to recruit highly skilled and highly paid employees in a variety of technical areas. To do so I have had to compete with places like Silicon Valley for talent. The Green Music Center is a significant cultural enhancement to the North Bay that will make it easier to recruit and retain these highly skilled people. A number of people I recruited to Sonoma County are now leading companies that are employing hundreds of people.

- Third and finally, as philanthropists, we wanted to help with a project that would benefit generations to come. We take for granted what our forefathers have built for us in the form of great libraries, concert halls, cathedrals and museums. This was our turn to make such a contribution. The Green Music Center and Weill Hall, by any standard, have met the challenge of creating a transformative place. We have succeeded in creating an incredible asset for many generations to come.

As I sat in the hall on the inaugural weekend I had two thoughts: One, we were hearing musical perfection (thank you, Lang Lang). As the beer commercial puts it, "It doesn't get any better than this." And two, I felt really pleased that Maureen and I played an instrumental role in creating such a beautiful place.

Top left:
Christopher and
Jeanne Dinno

Top right:
Donald and Maureen
Green

Bottom left:
Norma and Corrick
Brown

Bottom center:
Cherie and Keith Hughes

Bottom right:
Jerry Brown, Marne
Olson, Ruben Armiñana,
Anne Gust Brown

Top left:
Margaret Purser,
Jake Mackenzie

Top right:
Robert Rosen, Jeanne
Johnson, Miguel Ruelas

Center left:
Ajay and Ritu Banga

Center right:
Jan Shrem and
Maria Manetti

Bottom left:
Victoria Green Comfort
and son Nicholas

Bottom right:
Audrey and Barry
Sterling

Top left:
Brad and Corine
Bollinger, Jake and
Barbara Mackenzie

Top right:
Gina and Kevin Hunter

Center left:
Dr. and Mrs. Chuck
Young

Center right:
John and Gaye LeBaron

Bottom:
Larry and Karen
Furukawa-Schlereth

Top left:
Garret Gooch and
Mac Hart

Top right:
Connie Codding, Diane
Trembley, Viveka Rydell

Center left:
Jim Lamb and
daughter Garlane

Center right:
Tom Birdsall, Rebecca
Green Birdsall,
Duncan Birdsall

Bottom: Karin and
Anna Guzmán

Top left:
Bob Friend, Michelle Friend, Jack Lundgren, Suzanne Brangham

Top right:
Theresa and Alan Silow

Center left:
Lynn Woolsey

Center right:
Jackie Simons and Norma Person

Bottom:
Nancy Pelosi and Jerry Brown

Top left:
Sara Woodfield, Jeff
Langley, Peter Woodfield

Top right:
Arnie and Gayle Carston

Bottom left:
Erik and Ariann Greeny

Bottom right:
Barton Evans and
Andrea Neves

Schroeder Hall – A Special Gala Completes the Vision of Long Ago

Coming full circle, two years after Weill Hall's inauguration, Schroeder Hall opened its doors for a celebratory gala on August 22, 2014, and a community weekend August 23-24, featuring more than 100 artists in 10 free concerts. It was a glorious weekend that brought hundreds of community members who had never been to the Green Music Center to experience musical excellence in their own backyard.

SSU president Ruben Armiñana and community philanthropist Jean Schulz, who had allowed the hall to be named after the *Peanuts* cartoon boy pianist created by her husband, Charles, hoisted a huge scissors to cut the ribbon to open the hall officially for generations to come.

Highlights of the weekend included concerts by acclaimed pianist David Benoit, performing a Tribute to Charlie Brown; pianist, Santa Rosa Symphony Conductor Laureate, and Los Angeles Chamber Orchestra Music Director Jeffrey Kahane playing Beethoven and Chopin; recitals by Sonoma State University students and faculty; a christening of the hall's Brombaugh Opus 9 organ by James David Christie of the Boston Symphony Orchestra; and a capstone concert featuring Christie, soprano Ruth Ann Swenson, conductor Julian Wachner and the SSU Brass Ensemble.

It was a very exciting day for Jean Schulz (right) as Schroeder Hall officially launched on August 23, 2014, two years after Weill Hall opened.

Top: Visitors to Schroeder Hall, conceived as a choral music venue with narrow walls and a tall ceiling, enjoyed a performance by Bob Worth and the Bach Choir on Schroeder's inaugural weekend.

Bottom: Table dressings at the gala celebration featured items representing Schroeder and Jean and Charles Schulz.

In 2009, I arranged for California State Senator Mark Leno to visit the Green Center. He was very favorably impressed. We asked him if he knew Michael Tilson Thomas, music director of the San Francisco Symphony. Yes, the Senator knew him. Our next question: "Would you suggest that 'MTT' come here to see the facility?" At that juncture, the Senator pulled out his cell phone and we heard, "Mike? Mark. I'm at the new music hall at Sonoma State University and I think you'd be very interested in seeing this."

A year later, we were sitting in what would become Weill Hall, named after an amazing gift of $12 million from Joan and Sanford Weill, when the San Francisco Symphony let forth with the overture from Leonard Bernstein's Candide. As the brass and percussion music blasted through the audience, we all saw the joyous satisfaction registered on the Greens', the Browns' and the Armiñanas' proud and happy faces. The acoustics were astounding. We had done it—some more than others, yet all of us together. Later, I said to Marne Olson, "Congratulations! You are the only woman I know who has given birth to a concert hall." Oh happy day!

Steve Carroll

Philanthropist and Friend

Fireworks lit up the sky behind Weill Hall + Lawn during the grand finale of the 2015 July 4 fireworks spectacular concert featuring Broadway singer Megan Hilty and the Santa Rosa Symphony. The annual Independence Day celebration drew a crowd of more than 4,000 patrons both inside the hall and on the terraced lawn.

Finale

For many, the Green Music Center and Weill Hall have already surpassed expectations with world-class performers, bicoastal education programs, widespread financial support, enthusiastic audiences and international recognition. But these achievements come as no surprise to those responsible for where we are today.

> *We are the music makers, and we are the dreamers of dreams.*
> — Arthur O'Shaughnessy, British poet

The vision and sustaining leadership of Ruben Armiñana and Marne Olson, Donald and Maureen Green, Corrick and Norma Brown, and Joan and Sandy Weill have brought to fruition a long-held dream. The tireless efforts of the GMC team on the ground—led by Co-Executive Directors Larry Furukawa-Schlereth and Zarin Mehta—are shaping the direction of the Green Music Center, Weill Hall and Schroeder Hall.

It truly takes a village to imagine, create and run an operation as complex as the Green Music Center. The small but mighty team that made it happen: Jay Abbe, Kristin Berger, Robert Cole, Christopher Dinno, Robin Draper, Ryan Ernst, Erik Greeny, Anne Handley, Nate Johnson, Stuart Jones, Susan Kashack, Alan Kleinschmidt, Dan Lanahan, Jeff Langley, Ruth McDonnell, Lynn McIntyre, Patricia McNeill, Jim Meyer, Kamen Nikolov, Bucky Peterson, Sue Riley, Floyd Ross, Bruce Walker, Jean Wasp and Brian Wilson.

Those who continue to see to its success each and every day include Caroline Ammann, Lisa Andresen, Steven Berry, Adam Burkholder, Becky Cale, Terrell Cheney, Megan Christensen, Cindy Chong, Shaun Dayton, Robin Freeman, Lori Hercs, Jana Jackson, Kelley Kaslar, Kindra Kautz, Josef Keller, John Locher, Laura Lupei, Kathy Mahler, Pat Maloney, Neil Markley, Jessica Markus, Kevin Martin, Joseph McNiff, Sally Miller, Kamen Nikolov, Melissa Sanders, Cody Smith, Jerry Uhlig, Jessica Way and Ruth Wilson as well as the many students and volunteers involved with the Green Music Center.

Tribute must also be paid to the more than 1,800 individuals who generated $72 million in private donor support for the capital campaign, plus hundreds more who continue to support programming and operations.

What a ride!

Epilogue

It's hard to believe that more than three years have already passed since that grand September opening. The Green Music Center has grown, opening new venues and attracting new audiences, donors and artists with each passing year. Yet the vision—the guiding principle that carried this project from the seed of an idea to the world-class performing arts center that stands here today—has held strong. Our community has created a place where the arts and education thrive, and where culture comes to life.

Outstanding national and international performers continue to view the Green Music Center and Weill Hall as a most desirable venue. Audiences fill the seats inside the main hall and, when the back door is open, cover most of Weill Lawn and Terrace.

After the opening in September 2012, artists of distinction continue to fill Weill Hall with their extraordinary musicianship. Lang Lang and Yo-Yo Ma returned for a second year. The second season also included Renée Fleming, Josh Groban, Barbara Cook, Itzhak Perlman, Herbie Hancock, the Vienna Philharmonic Orchestra, Ruth Ann Swenson, Hilary Hahn, Deborah Voigt, Bryn Terfel, Jason Mraz and more.

> *Music gives a soul to the universe, wings to the mind, flight to the imagination and life to everything.*
>
> — Plato

In 2013, Zarin Mehta, former president of the New York Philharmonic, was named co-executive director, sharing the position with Sonoma State CFO and Vice President for Administration and Finance Larry Furukawa-Schlereth.

A wildly popular Summer 2014 season brought musical greats to Sonoma County such as Tony Bennett, Frankie Valli, Diana Ross, the San Francisco Symphony and others.

Mehta, with his keen understanding of music and decades of industry experience—from the Montreal Symphony to Chicago's Ravinia Festival, and a celebrated tenure at the Philharmonic—quickly made his mark on the artistic vision of the Green Music Center, launching a season that showcased a vast variety of artistic genres throughout the 2014-15 season, the most musically diverse and culturally rich lineup thus far seen in Weill Hall.

He also oversaw the opening of the new Schroeder Hall in August 2014, with a weekend of diverse concerts that celebrated the venue's unique attributes—such as the stunning Brombaugh Opus 9 tracker organ installed on a loft above the stage—and highlighted the talented faculty and staff of Sonoma State University, in addition to acclaimed artists including David Benoit, Jeffrey Kahane and James David Christie.

The 2014-15 season features stellar artists including Michael Feinstein, Johnny Mathis, Emerson String Quartet, Ramsey Lewis and Cécile McLorin Salvant, Audra McDonald, Jeffrey Kahane, Bobby McFerrin, Anne-Sophie Mutter, Murray Perahia and many others.

The future certainly looks bright for the Green Music Center.

The Green Music Center Board of Advisors

While the inaugural season began to take shape, the leadership and vision of the organization was also flourishing. With Sandy Weill as chairman, the newly developed Green Music Center Board of Advisors had attracted entrepreneurs, philanthropists and community leaders from Wine Country and beyond. By the close of the inaugural season, the Board of Advisors had grown from a handful of dedicated visionaries to a robust group of more than 20 arts advocates.

The general purpose of the Board of Advisors of the Green Music Center is to help ensure the future and continuity and to further the mission of the Green Music Center. The Board assists the Green Music Center through giving financial support, providing advocacy on behalf of the organization, and serving as an advisor to the Green Music Center's management. The Green Music Center is committed to excellence in artistic and educational programming; to commissioning new work and presenting important premieres; to exploring the full range of the performing arts in its many disciplines and from diverse cultures; and to providing education through programs in the community for people of all ages and through its academic role on campus.

Appendix

Donald & Maureen Green Music Center Capital Campaign Donor Honor Roll

From the time the Green Music Center vision was born through the many years it grew and took hold, there were more than 1,800 donors who said yes to its possibilities, giving in ways large and small to ensure its future.

$1,000,000 and above

In memory of Ruth Garland Bowes
Herb and Jane Dwight
Donald and Maureen Green
G. K. Hardt
Don C. and Louise S. Johnston,
    in memory of David Charles Johnston
MasterCard
Norma and Evert Person
Jacques and Barbara Schlumberger
Jean and Charles Schulz
Santa Rosa Symphony
Trione Foundation
Les and Judy Vadasz, Vadasz Family Foundation
John and Jennifer Webley
Joan and Sanford I. Weill and the
    Weill Family Foundation

$500,000 - $999,999

B.J. and Bebe Cassin
Koret Foundation
Sonne J. Pedersen
Santa Rosa Symphony League
Edward and Carolyn Stolman Foundation
Holly and Henry Wendt

$100,000 - $499,999

Kären and Jay Abbe
Advanced Fibre Communications
Bank of America Charitable Foundation
Mike and Foster Beigler
The Bippart Family
Tom Birdsall and Rebecca Green Birdsall
Lawrence Broderick
Corrick and Norma Brown and Family
Arnie and Gayle Carston/World of
    Carpet One
Hugh and Connie Codding

Nancy Doyle, MD, and George L. Smith, Jr., MD
Charles and Deborah Eid
Eschelon Telecom
Exchange Bank
Tom and Betty Freeman
Michelle and Robert Friend
Laurence K. Gould, Jr.
Victoria Green Comfort
Guerrera Family
Deborah and Michael Hatfield
Douglas P. Heen and William A. Scogland
The William and Flora Hewlett Foundation
In memory of Juelle and Allen Hinman
Jackson Family Wines
Jack V. and Marilyn R. Jones
Sandra Jordan
Tom Jordan
Jim and Charlotte Lamb
Maribelle and Stephen Leavitt
Nancy and Tony Lilly
Neil and Amelia McDaniel Charitable Trust
Gary D. and Marcia L. Nelson
OCLI/a JDS Uniphase Company
Joan Ramsay Palmer
The Family of Estelle Ratner
Eric Rossin and Beth Weisburn
Roxy and Kathleen Roth
Marv and Fran Soiland
Stuart Davidson Squair
Wayne and Gladys Valley Foundation
Harry and Margaret Wetzel
Bill and Pat White
Joseph C. Zils Family Fund

$50,000 - $99,999

Friends of the Green Music Center

Lindsay and Kirsten Austin

In memory of Roger Barber

Anne and Dan Benedetti

Ajaib Singh and Sukhninder Kaur Bhadare

Ellen De Martini

Hallie and Paul Downey

Ms. Fay Gallus and Dr. Richard Sweet

James W. Gavagan

Robert Gilchrist, in memory of Gay Kenny

Arthur and Lynda Matney

Margaret McCarthy and Robert Worth

Merrill Lynch

Laurence Lusk Moore Charitable Trust

Bob and Carole Nicholas

The Joseph and Evelyn Rosenblatt
    Charitable Fund

Irwin and Coleen Rothenberg, Wealth
    Management Consultants, LLC

Dry Creek Vineyard and David S. Stare

Temple Family Trust

Hugh Trutton

John and Terry Votruba

Peter and Sara Woodfield

$25,000 - $49,999

Friends of the Green Music Center

Anderson, Zeigler, Disharoon, Gallagher & Gray

William C. and Ann M. Anderson

Ruben Armiñana and Marne J. Olson

Jane and Gerald Baldwin

James and Joann Berger

Ann and Gordon Blumenfeld

Berenice and Lawrence Brackett

Ginger and Sam Brown

Gary and Charlene Bunas

Francisco Canales, MD, and
    Heather Furnas, MD

Linda Castiglioni

Patti and Ray Chambers

Pamela and Timothy Chanter

Clover-Stornetta Farms

Jess and Crawford Cooley

Marcia Da Pont, in memory of
    Richard Hastings Da Pont

Joan Withers Dinner, in memory of
    Richard S. Dinner

Pete Dintiman

Family and friends, in memory of Bill Donaldson

Darlene Donaldson Family

Nancy and Dale Dougherty

Sheila and Harold Einhorn,
    in honor of our parents

Stanley A. Feingold and Roslyn Edelson

Fornage Family

Lynn and Claude Ganz

Joseph A. and Judith M. Gappa

Jan Gilman of the Lenore and
    Howard Klein Foundation

Paul M. and Marcia H. Ginsburg

Hansel Auto Group

Sandy and Cindy Harris

Stu Harrison and Dave Ring

Jim and Betty Huhn

Gene Jemail and Betty Joslyn Jemail

Martha and Jeffrey Kahane

Michael and Karen Kasper

Louis and Olivia Kendall

The Kornfeld Family, in memory of Ann Abeles

Edward and Elizabeth Kozel, Sr.

Jim and Linda Kuhns, in honor of
    Charlotte Lamb

James H. L'Hommedieu

Dan Lanahan and Martin Reilley

Lawrence and Frances Lok and Family

Frank and Kathleen Mayhew

Hannah Rose McNeely, Rosemary McNeely,
    Kevin McNeely

Greg and Laura Mlynarczyk

Melissa Monson

Tim and Nancy Muller

The Charles Murphy Family

Ron and Eileen Nelson

Nadenia Newkirk

Delphine Newman

Estate of Paul Nielsen

Paul D. O'Connor

The Reverend Francis and Mary O'Reilly

Steve Osborn, Renata Breth, Celeste Osborn

Joyce and Steve Pease

Marty and Ken Prouty

Chuck and Kati Quibell

Republic Services, Inc.

Floyd Ross, in memory of
    William and Virginia Ross

William and Joan Roth

Santa Rosa Symphony Musicians and Staff

Santa Rosa Symphony Musicians from the
    Corrick Brown Fund

Robert and Joan Scheel

Schurter Inc.

Mr. and Mrs. Andrew J. Shepard

Irene and David Sohm

Sonoma State University Alumni Association

Shirley Spencer

State Farm Companies Foundation

The Audrey and Barry Sterling Family of
    Iron Horse Vineyards

Charles and Maryanna Stockholm

David and Vicki Stollmeyer

Jane and Jack Stuppin

J. F. and Susan S. Taylor

Mrs. Edward J. Throndson

William M. Vick and Susan Lee Vick

Renee Vollen

Michael J. Waldorf

Rod and Lynne Wallace

David Walls and Barbara Walls Hanson,
    in memory of Elizabeth S. Walls

Robert H. Walter Family Trust

Wells Fargo Bank

Creighton and Dorothy White

Annette and Rick Wilber

Michael and Katie Wright

$10,000 – $24,999

Friends of the Green Music Center

Janice Grace Adams

Jizell Albright

Gerald S. Anderson and Beatrice N. Coxhead

Joe and Phyllis Apfel

Julie and Tom Atwood

Chuck and Dorothy Aver

John and Ruth Baillie

Gary and Maria Baldwin

Frank and Grace Barner

Chester Beck, Paul Dillon and Jack Murphy

Richard and Pamela Beebe

Milo and Marj Bell

Gene and Evelyn Benedetti

Timothy and Corey Benjamin

Roberta Gourse Berg, MD

Nancy and David Berto

Dr. Kate Black

The Blades Family

Don Bradley, for Ted and Helen Zoe

Sanford and Jo Anne Bressick

Keven Brown and Jeri Yamashiro Brown

Mark Burchill and MeL Konrad

Tom and Elinor Burnside

Barbara Butler and Jim Ford

To honor the Cahn and Bennett Families

Mrs. Grant W. Canfield

Carle, Mackie, Power & Ross LLP

Laura Chenel and John Van Dyke

Ken and Darlene Christiansen

Helen M. Clasper

William and Sara Clegg, in memory of
    Dr. Harding Clegg

Patricia F. Clothier

Ellen and Louis Comaduran

Nan and Ransom Cook

John K. and Katharyn W. Crabbe

Jack and Beverly Cranston

Terry and Joanne Dale

Chet and Noelle Dangremond

In memory of Flora Dean

Dr. and Mrs. Thomas C. Degenhardt

Didi and Pershing DeGolia

Jayne DeLawter and Kenneth Koppelman

Edward and Bernice Dermott

Ron and Kris Dick

Peggy Donovan-Jeffry and John J. Jeffry

Robin A. Draper and Mike Davis

Mary and Eric Drew

Jack Dupre and Marsha Vas Dupre

E.A. Durell & Co. Inc.

Kate Ecker and John Mackie

Paul and Mary Elliott

Edward and Joanne Enemark

Kathleen Nanette Ferrington and Brent Finley

Dr. Richard and Barbara Ferrington

Fireman's Fund Insurance Company

Fred and Juelle Fisher

Pauline "Polly" Fisher

Ned and Sally Foley

Lewis and Diana Forney

Dr. and Mrs. Jacob J. Foster

Anne and John Friedemann

Patricia and William Fuller

Larry and Karen Furukawa-Schlereth

Cappie and Tom Garrett

Richard and Jennifer Girvin

Pat Glasner Family, in memory of Mary "Taffy"
    Glasner and Kevin Glasner

Karen Godfrey and Richard Israel

Steve Goldberg and Renee Miguel

Richard and Rhoda Goldman Fund

Bernie and Estelle Goldstein

Jule Grant, in honor of Dr. Susan McKillop, Dr.
    Robert Jefferson, Dr. Gardner Rust

John and Pamela Graziano, in memory of Dot
    Drew and Joe Marasco

Lawrence Guernsey Family Trust

John and Jean Hackenburg

Ann Hall

William K. Hamilton

In memory of Chod Harris VP2ML WB2CHO

Jim and Jean Harrison and Keir Skinner

Judge Patricia Herron (Ret.)

Henry H. and Gloria Fabe Hersch

Spence and Anne Hiatt

Helen R. Higby, in memory of Ruth and
    Nick Higby

Ruth V. Hosty

Rick and Geri Johnston

Samuel L. Jones and Candace P. Jones

Janet and Bo Kirschen

Sara and Edward Kozel

Diane Krause and Gerrett Snedaker

Antoinette Kuhry and Thomas Haeuser

Peter and Exine Lamonica

In memory of Bruce S. Lane and
    Mary Ellen Lane

Jeff Langley, in honor of Leonard and
    Judith Kertzner

Eugenia Lea-McKenzie

The Leavens Foundation

Louisa Leavitt

Dan G. and Carol L. Libarle

Joanne and Glenn Lillich

Jim Lotter, in memory of Gladys V. Lotter

Maria Elizabeth Lucidi

Darrell Luperini DDS and Chantal Vogel

Dale Lynch and Joanne Foote Lynch

Michael MacDonald

Catherine and David Marsten

John and Pat Martin

Henry and Diane Mayo

Kai-Uwe Mazur, MD, and Lindsay Mazur

Louise and William B. McCann

Gerald and Lynn McIntyre

Patricia McNeill and Gabriela Schwenker

Clifford and Patty Melim

Jim and Shirley Meyer

Gene and Carole Michel

William and Julie Middleton

Syd and Judy Miller

Richard Morehead, Jr., and Kenneth Knight

Barbara Moulton, in memory of
    Charity H. Morse

Douglas and Barbara Murray

Lorna and Neil Myers

Jim and Gwen Neary

Daniel Needham

Gary and Elsa Nelson

Phyllis Steinman Caplan Nesbitt and
    Douglas Nesbitt

Robert and Sally Nicholson

Eric and Yvonne Norrbom

Cissie and Mid O'Brien

Michael Panas, in memory of
    Elaine "Honey" Panas

Dorothy B. Pathman

Clare Pearson, MD, in honor of
    Kathryn and Kent

Judith S. Peletz

Beverly J. Perry

Monika and Peter Piasecki

Pisenti & Brinker LLP

The Putney Financial Group

Damon and Marjorie Raike

William H. and Barbara Ramsey

John and Susan Reed

Bill and Mary-Louise Reinking

Dr. Robert and Barbara Richardson

Jonathan M. Riley

Sharon and Jerry Robison

Ira H. and Ruth S. Rosenberg

Harry L. Rubins

Martha Rapp Ruddell and Perry M. Marker

William J. and Helen B. Rudee

David L. and Sandra J. Sandine

Carol Cochran Schaffner

William M. and Marilyn P. Schlangen

Susan and Dale Schmid

Diane Schoenrock

John and Gayle Schofield

Bruno H. Schurter

Dr. and Mrs. W. McFate Smith

Sonoma Bank

Alan Soule

Walter and Mary Spellman

Kathleen Spitzer and Stephen C. Miller

Rich and Laura Stanfield

Dr. Michael Star

Gregory and Patricia Steele

Marlene and Martin Stein

Cornelia Sulzer

Judith Croll Swanger

Earle and Terri Sweat

Barry Swenson Builder

Roselyne Chroman Swig

Michele and Scott Thayer

Sigrid Thomason and Hedy Stut

Tietz Family Foundation

Dr. and Mrs. Alessandro Trombetta

Michael Troy and Judy Shubin

Evelyn Niemack Truman, in memory of
    Robert V. Truman

L. Stephen and Neva Turer

Ransom and Marilyn Turner

Arlene and Joseph Ulmer

Alice and Lloyd von der Mehden

Shirley and Bill Ward

Ron Welch and Ellen Watson

Janet and Patrick Wentworth

Matt and Melissa White

Constance Wolfe and Marshall Kent

Robert and Donna Young

Kirt and Bev Zeigler

Beryl F. Zimberoff, in memory of
    Michael J. Fasman

$5,000 - $9,999

Friends of the Green Music Center

Yale and Terry Abrams

Ammons Family

Carolyn J. Anderson

Bob and Karin Andrews

Jack Atkins and Yvonne Darling-Atkins

Carol Babcock, in memory of
    Donald S. Babcock

William and Karen Babula, in memory of
    Joseph A. Gemi

Catherine Bachman

Richard Barbieri, in memory of
    Mary Ann Barbieri

Chuck Bartley

Bauers and Keenans, in memory of
    Elizabeth K. Bauer, PhD

Dr. and Mrs. Jeffrey D. Bean

Donn and Patricia Bearden

In memory of Eleanor Bearden

Stephen and Terry Beck

Dr. and Mrs. Bruce M. Bell

Gail and Barry Ben-Zion

Beyers|Costin

Barbara Biebush

John Boland and James Carroll

Brad and Corine Bollinger

John and Sandy Bond

Ryan C. Bradley

Suzanne Brangham and Jack Lundgren

Elva J. Brinegar

The Corrick Brown family, in memory of
    Stan Diamond

In loving memory of LaVerna Brown

The Browns, in memory of Dorothy McGuire

Robert F. Brown, in memory of
    Katherine L. Cleveland-Brown

Bertie and Robert Brugge

Richard and Karin Burger

Thera A. Buttaro

The Chan-Stanek Family

F. Scott and Shirley Chilcott

Tom and Irene Clark

Clay Foundation - West

Kim and Clay Clement

Harold L. Coleman and Alice S. Coleman

Michael and Mary Colhoun

Dan and Janet Condron

Steven and Geraldine Congdon

Edward and Nancy Conner

Randolph W. and Jean W. Cornes

Mr. and Mrs. Kim and Michelle Covington

Wilson Craig

Mrs. W. A. Dager

Rocky L. Daniels and Deborah W. Trefz

Susan and Fred David

Chris and Bonnie Day

John and Nancy Dayton

Anne and Edward Del Monte

Raul and Nancy Diez

Carolyn Doran and Lawrence Shapiro

James and Jean Douglas

Gordon and Joanne Dow

Donors and Friends, in honor of Robin Draper

Timothy and Gloria Oster Duncan

Charles A. Dunkel

Randon and Juliana Duranceau

Karen Dutton and George R. Dutton

Winston and Louann Ekren

Ted and Peggy Elliott

Robert and Dolores Evans

Whitney and Jeanette P. Evans

Harry W. Fall and Barbara J. Fall

Mary and Scott Farrar

In memory of Martin and Elisabeth Feinman

Dr. Reed and Nancy Ferrick

Mildred Ferro, in memory of Michael O. Ferro

Jeanne Ferroggiaro

Herbert M. Fougner

Charles and Perry Freeman

Gene and Marjorie Friedrich

Bob and Rita Frugoli

Gary Garabedian

Robert and Terese Gilford

Mr. and Mrs. C. Convers Goddard

Leona and Joel Green

Florence Gresty

Karin Guzmán, in memory of Raoul Guzmán

Ray and Amanda Haas

Dick and Mary Hafner

Marty Hamilton, in memory of
    Beverly Hamilton

William and Constance Hammerman

Jim and Anne Handley

Alyce Hansel

Jack F. Harper and Deyea V. Harper

William C. and Doris E. Harrison

Marta Hayden, in memory of Blanche Hayden
    and Carmen Roberts

Mr. and Mrs. Robert Hayden

Sally L. Heath

Professor Bryant and Mrs. Diane Hichwa

James and Carolyn Hinton

John and Joan Hodge

Bruce and Elizabeth Hoelter

Jean Holm Shell

John A. Holt and Geraldine P. Holt

Herbert and Lois Howe

Keith and Cherie Hughes

Gary and Lynn Imm

Jeff and Judy James and Family

Dr. and Mrs. Nathan Johnson

David and Ann Jones

Malcolm Jones and Karen Roche

Michael and Susan Kashack

Arthur and Judith Kayen

Keegan & Coppin Company, Inc.

John and Jan Kern

Kiwanis Club of Santa Rosa Suburban

Katharine and Jean-Serge Klein

Martha G. Köhn

Lorraine Komor, in memory of Peter S. Komor

Lily Krulevitch, in memory of Tova and
    Max Fishman

Dennis E. Lantz, in memory of
    Lawrence L. Lantz

Judge Henry B. and Bonnie Lasky

Richard and Dianne Leger

Lemo USA, Inc.

Stephanie Leong and Raymond Tom

Amy Miller Levine and Joel R. Levine, MD

Millie G. Libarle

Sid and Gerry Lipton

Barney and Cindy Locke

Anne and Alexander Long

John and Joan Lounsbery

Richard C. Ludmerer

Malkemus family, in honor of Annabelle George

Kitty and Fred Mann

Richard and Caroline Marker

Drs. David and Norma Marks

Valerie J. Marshall and Mark A. Matthews

Jane Mastick

Mr. and Mrs. Jack W. McCarley

John and Evelyn McClure

Neil and Amelia McDaniel

George and Marie McKinney

Jean McLaughlin

Laura Kimble McLellan

James Stewart Miller

James and Joann Mitchell

Patricia Moehlman, in memory of
    Shirley Sparling

Doug Morton and Paula Jackson

Madi and Robert Mount

Alan and Dorothy Murray

Warren and Elizabeth Musser

The Neal Family

Manuel and Cynthia Nestle

H. Andrea Neves and Barton Evans

Charles Nevil and Nancy Bleiweiss-Nevil

Bruce and Sindy Nevins

Barbara and Ambrose R. Nichols, Jr.

Susan and Philip Nix

David Noorthoek, MD

Gloria Ogg and David Bates

Nancy Ogg, in memory of Gilbert "Tim" Foote

John and Kirsten Olney

Steve and Lynn Olsen, in memory of the Price
    and Olsen Families

David and Aggie Olson

Paul and Sandra Otellini, in honor of
    Alexis Otellini

Raul and Diana Paabo

Louise Packard and Larry Moskowitz

Harriet and Bernard Palk

William A. Payne and Sandra J. Settle

Dr. Charles and Margaret Peck

Fred J. Pedersen

Tom and JaMel Perkins

Glenn and Jana Peterson

The Family of Katherine Pew, in her honor

Douglas Pinter and David Young

Joan and Lewis Platt

Richard Pratt and Kathie Murphy

Virginia Pyke

Joseph A. and Mary E. Rattigan

Gail Reid, for her father, Leland Chapman

Harry and Dee Richardson

Betty and Herb Riess

Kenneth Ripple and Peggy Morris

David and Vicki Ritter

C. Beth Robertson

Rabbi Michael A. and Ruth Robinson

Emily and Walter Roeder

Venetta and John P. Rohal

Jack and Katie Rohrman for Florence R. Lamb

Michele Rosen

E. G. Rust

George S. Sarlo

Denise Scaglione

Ralph and Janice Sceales

Doris Schaefer

Richard and Ann Schindler

Bob and Priscilla Schultz

Jean and Ian Seddon

Raymond N. Shapiro, MD

Harvey and Deborah Shein

Michelle Sikora

Vernon and Lida Simmons

Robert W. and Rachel M. Sinai

Susan K. Skinner and Robert G. Heisterberg

Larry and Zilpha Snyder

Roslyn Squair, in memory of Stuart and
    Jean Squair

Jon and Teresita Stark

Kathleen and David Steadman

In memory of Kathleen R. Steadman by family
    and friends

Gay B. and Hans L. Stern

Margaret Stock

Stoesser-Gordon Plastics

Gillian and Ross Stromberg

Roy and Emily Stubbs

Summit State Bank

Joanne and John Taylor

Waights Taylor and Liz Martin

Mrs. Walter J. Treanor, in memory of
    Dr. Treanor

Joe and Eunice Valentine

The Veritys, in memory of
    Frances Barrick Verity

Michael and Janet Verlander

Dr. and Mrs. Eric W. Vetter

Robert and Catherine Vila

Vineyard Creek Hotel

Terry and Cristina Wadsworth

Victor Waithman, in memory of
    Norma Waithman

In loving memory of Bruce R. Walker

Marilyn and Edward Wallis

Dr. and Mrs. Richard Wallrich

Mrs. Joan Walsh

Dotty and Jim Walters

Jane and Nelson Weller

Greg and Gay Wilcox

Zeanette Williams

Elizabeth B. Witchey, in memory of
    Julian C. Ryer and Mary F. Holme

Scott and Lee Wright

Tim and Pam Zainer

Shirlee Zane and Peter Kingston

John and Dayna Van-Kleeck Ziegler

$1 - $4,999

Mr. Robert J. Abbey

Mr. Winfield Achor

Mr. Harry Adams

Ms. Elaine T. Adamson

Ms. Sheila P. Albert

Mr. Wilbur D. Albright

Dr. Dolores Ali

All Golfers Tour Association

Ms. Gail Allen and Ms. Susan Allen

Mr. and Mrs. John Allen

Mr. and Mrs. Paul H. Allen, Jr.

Alliance Capital Management

Ms. Dorcas Allison

Ms. Phyllis A. Allison

Dr. and Mrs. Richard Altimari

Ms. Edith Amateau

Ms. Joan Ambrosini

American AgCredit ACA

American Legion - Healdsburg Post 111

Amici's East Coast Pizzeria

Ms. Ann E. Amyes

Mr. and Mrs. Allan Anderson

Mr. and Mrs. Brad Anderson

Mrs. Jeanne Anderson

Ms. Roberta R. Anderson

Mr. and Mrs. Samuel G. Anderson

Ms. Ann Andrews

Ms. Frances A. Andrews

Ms. Marilyn Ansel

Dr. and Mrs. Milton A. Antipa

Dr. and Mrs. Nicholas H. Anton

Mr. and Mrs. Paul Archambeau

Mr. Hollace Archer

Ms. Winifred Archibald

Ms. Carolyn Ardalan

Ms. Mary Armstrong and
   Ms. Christy Armstrong

Mr. and Mrs. Tom Arnott

Mr. Jeremy Arroyo

AT&T Foundation Matching Gift Program

Ms. Jean Atkinson

Ms. Adrien Avis

B.S.I. Insurance Services

Mr. and Mrs. Aldo Baccala

John Bagley Jewelry Gallery

Ms. Dolores Bailey

Mr. George Baker

Ms. Patricia Baker

Mr. and Mrs. Robert E. Baker

Ms. Sheyna Bakman

Dr. Michael E. Baldigo

Mr. and Mrs. Michael W. Baldus

Ms. Marlene G. Ballaine

Mr. and Mrs. Fred Baltonado

Dr. and Mrs. Mussa Banisadre

Mr. and Mrs. Daniel Bargar

Ms. Marjorie Barnebey

Mr. and Mrs. Ben Barnes

Dr. Robert Baron

Mr. Clay H. Barr

Mr. David A. Barr and Mrs. Helen Sharritt

Mr. and Mrs. John P. Barry

Ms. Arline Bastien

Mr. Douglas G. Bates

Mr. and Mrs. Alfred Batzdorff

Mr. and Mrs. John Baum

Mr. and Mrs. Michael S. Baum

Mr. and Mrs. Alfred L. Baumann

Mr. and Mrs. Frank H. Baumgardner

Ms. Margery T. Baur

Ms. Mary K. Beatty

Dr. Irene Becker

Mr. and Mrs. David Beckman

Ms. Marcea Bedayan

Ms. June C. Beebe

Ms. Marie Belden

Ms. Diantha D. Bell

Mr. and Mrs. James R. Benefield

Dr. and Mrs. David W. Benson

Ms. Lois Benson

Ms. Sharron Bentley

Mr. and Mrs. Thomas N. Bentley

Mr. William Berentz

Mr. and Mrs. Robert Berg

Mr. and Mrs. Tom Berger

Mr. and Mrs. Steve P. Bernard

Ms. Rhoda Bernie

Ms. Johanna Berthowd

Mr. William S. Bertram

Mr. and Mrs. Steve Betterly

Ms. Barbara M. Biggs

Mr. Vernon Birks

Dr. and Mrs. George W. Bisbee

David and Sabrina Bjornstrom

Black Dog Private Foundation

Mr. and Mrs. Don Black

Mr. and Mrs. Arnold L. Bloom

Mr. Richard D. Bloom and Ms. Bridget McCoy

Mr. and Mrs. Joel Blumenfeld

Ms. Margaret E. Bock

Mrs. Stephanie Bodi-Gaffney and
   Mr. Joe Gaffney

Dr. Russell J. Bodner

Ms. Rosemary E. Boezi

Ms. Patricia L. Bolton

Mr. William R. Boorman

Mr. and Mrs. Stanley J. Borges

Ms. Virginia C. Borggaard

Mr. and Mrs. Robert Bortolotto

Mr. Al Bosch and Mrs. Jaquelin Tomke-Bosch

Mr. and Mrs. L. M. Boss

Ms. Mary S. Boster

Mr. and Mrs. Ronald L. Bosworth

Ms. Carolyn Boughton

Ms. Joyce Bowen

Ms. Sandra Bowler

Mr. and Mrs. Obie Bowman

Ms. Florence Boxerman

BP Foundation, Inc.

Mr. and Mrs. Michael Brady

Mr. Charles Brandner

Ms. Becky Brandt

Ms. Evelyn Breger

Bridgeworks

Ms. Edythe M. Briggs and Mr. Robert Carrithers

Mr. and Mrs. Clifton Brinkley

Ms. and Mr. Demaris Brinton

Mr. and Mrs. Seymour M. Brody

Mrs. Barbara A. Brooks and Dr. Floyd L. Brooks

Mr. and Mrs. Frederic A. Brossy, Jr.

Mr. and Mrs. Dixon Browder

Mr. and Mrs. Cameron M. Brown

Mr. and Mrs. Frank B. Brown

Mr. and Mrs. Jefferson Brown

Ms. Marie Browne

Mr. and Mrs. Phillip B. Brownell

Law Offices of Thomas M. Bruen

Dr. and Mrs. Joe H. Brumbaugh

Ms. Rose Bucchianeri

Mr. and Mrs. Bruce Budner

Ms. Elise D. Bulger

Ms. Nancy E. Bullock

Ms. Marcia E. Burkart

Mr. and Mrs. Robert Burke

Mr. and Mrs. Robert Burness

Mr. H. G. Burns

Mr. and Mrs. Stephen L. Bursch

Mr. and Mrs. James Buskirk

Andy Butler

Mr. Joel Butler

Ms. Pamela Butler and Ms. Mary L. Butler

Mr. and Mrs. Sean Butler

Ms. Susan V. Butler

Ms. Cynthia G. Butner

Ms. Eugenia P. Butts

Mr. Steven M. Caccia

Mr. and Mrs. Alvin Cadd

Mr. and Mrs. John Cairns

Ms. Nancy Cameron

Ms. Alison Campbell

Ms. Doris Campbell

Ms. Elizabeth Campbell

June Campbell

Ms. Miloslava Capek

Ms. Adeline L. Carlson

Mr. and Mrs. Robert Carpenter

Mr. Michael J. Carroll and Ms. Linda M. Davis

Mr. Stephen E. Carroll and Mr. Charles J. Maisel

Ms. Birgit Carstensen

Mr. and Mrs. Jack Carter

Mr. and Mrs. M. V. Caruana

Mr. and Mrs. Jim Casciani

Louise Castle

Mr. James Caudill

Mr. and Mrs. William Cedar

Chambers and Chambers Wine

Mr. and Mrs. LeRoy Chandler

Chevron

Chevron Matching Gift

Mr. and Mrs. Bruce Chrisp

Mr. and Mrs. Donald L. Christie

Cisco Foundation

Ms. Beatryce Clark

Mr. and Mrs. Jack L. Clark

Mrs. Cindy Clayton

Mr. and Mrs. Robert F. Clazie

Mr. James E. Clegg and Ms. Lisa Bartlett

Mr. and Mrs. Robert C. Clement

Ms. Helen G. Clopton and Mr. Frank Slupesky

Dr. and Mrs. Galen E. Clothier

Cobb Insurance Services

Mr. Albert Cognata

Mr. Glenn Colacurci

Columbia Distributing Company

Colvin Group

Community Smart Program

Mr. and Mrs. Harrison F. Comstock

Mr. and Mrs. William E. Comstock

Mr. and Mrs. John Conley

Mr. and Mrs. Kevin F. Connolly

Mr. and Mrs. Craig Cook

Ms. Cynthia Cook and Mr. Ken Ackerman

Don Cook

Mr. Michael Cookson and Ms. Darcie Lamond

Copperfield's Books - Petaluma

Mr. and Mrs. Richard Corbett

Ms. Theodora Corroon

Mr. and Mrs. C. Thorne Corse

Dr. and Mrs. Hyland Cort

Costeaux French Bakery

Mr. and Mrs. Jim Cotton

Ms. Janet J. Coulter

Mr. Jeff Cox and Ms. Susanna M. Napierala-Cox

Mr. and Mrs. Sandy Craig

Max Cramer

Janice Craw

Ms. Ann M. Cress

Mr. and Mrs. Tom Croft

Ms. Dora E. Crowther

Mr. and Mrs. James H. Cummings II

Ms. Barbara L. Curry

Mr. and Mrs. Leonard C. Curry

Mr. and Mrs. Jerome Cutler

Mr. and Mrs. Richard Cutler

Mr. Mark Czepiel and Ms. Amy Paul

Ms. Caressa A. Da Roza

Mr. and Mrs. R. E. Dale

Mr. and Mrs. Robert J. Dana

Mr. and Mrs. Casey D'Angelo

Ms. Nancy J. Danskin

Ms. Mary Davenport

Ms. Claire K. Davis

Mr. and Mrs. Edward L. Davis II

Mr. and Mrs. Henry Davis

Dr. and Mrs. Michael A. Davis

Mr. and Mrs. M. Edgar Deas

Ms. Patricia DeBernardi

Mr. and Mrs. Vernon DeBernardi

Mr. and Mrs. Mike D'Elicio

Mr. and Mrs. Robert Dempel

Mr. and Mrs. Andre Dermant

Mr. and Mrs. Manuel G. Diaz

Mr. and Mrs. Alan DiCicco

Mr. and Mrs. Robert E. Dickerson

Ms. Linda J. Dickinson

Ms. Phyllis Diebenkorn

Dierk's Parkside Café

Mr. Warren Dietrich

Marvin and Bernadine Dillon

Ms. Susan S. Dillon

Mr. A. Barr Dolan

Mr. and Mrs. Marvin Dolowitz

Mr. and Mrs. James P. Donahue

Ms. Greta Dorfman

Mr. Ronald S. Douglass

The Dow Chemical Company Foundation

Mr. Joseph Dragony and Mrs. V. Meier-Dragony

Mrs. Prudence Draper

Mr. and Mrs. William Draper

Mr. and Mrs. Jerry Droll

Mr. and Mrs. George Duerr

Mr. and Mrs. Rene F. DuFour

Mr. Robert G. Duncan

Ms. Brigitte A. Dunn

Ms. Maria B. Dwight

Mr. Boyd K. Dyer

Mr. and Mrs. Bruce J. Dzieza

Mr. and Mrs. Nicholas Eagan

Ms. Margie Early

Ms. Sue Earnest

Lelia M. Eastburn

Ms. Linda K. Easterbrook

Ms. Valerie J. Easton

Virginia G. Eaton

Mr. Joseph Edelberg

Dr. Terry L. Eggleston

Dr. and Mrs. Charles Eichler

Jeff and Mary Eid

Ms. Patricia P. Eliot

Mrs. Linda Emblen

Ms. Kathleen A. Emery

Ms. Rosemary A. Endicott

Ms. Nancy England

Enterprise Rent-A-Car

Dr. and Mrs. Joel Erickson

Ms. Lynette Erlach

J.D. Escaturban

Mr. and Mrs. Todd Evans

Ms. Marietta Everitt

Ms. Nora Everson

Mr. Charles R. Ewald

Ms. Anne Facto

Mr. Chris Fadeff

Mr. Douglas Faigin and Ms. Mary J. Pew

Mr. Thomas Fairhurst

Dr. Yvette M. Fallandy

Mrs. Arthur J. Fallon

Ms. Elizabeth Farrar

Federated Department Stores

Ms. Joann E. Feldman

Mr. and Mrs. Norman Feldman

Dr. Phyllis M. Fernlund

Walter and Marie Filippi

Mr. and Mrs. James B. Findley

Mr. Dan Finkle and Mrs. Amy B. Gannon-Finkle

Mr. Kenneth Fischang

Mr. and Mrs. Charles H. Fischer

Mr. Sol Fishman

Mr. and Ms. David Flanagan

Ms. Judith A. Flowers

Mr. Edmond Fong

Mr. and Mrs. Art Ford

Lew and Diana Forney

Mr. and Mrs. William Foshee

Ms. Helen H. Foster

Terry Foster

Mr. and Mrs. W. R. Foster

Ms. Zelma Fouts

Ms. Louise Z. Fraley

Ms. Patricia A. Francis

Mr. and Mrs. Jon Fredrikson

Mr. and Mrs. Charles Freeman

Mr. and Mrs. James S. Frey

Ms. Natalie W. Friedman

Johanna E. Fritsche

Mr. Christopher A. Fritzsche

Martella and George Fry

Lawrence and Karen Fuller

Mr. and Mrs. Ed Fullerton

Michael and Nancy Funk

Furth Family Foundation

Mr. and Mrs. Daniel J. Galvin

Mr. and Mrs. Gary E. Gannon

Ms. Deborah Garber and Mr. Ronald M. Miska

Mr. and Mrs. John Gardner

Mr. and Mrs. R. S. I. Gardner

Ms. Janet Gartner

Dr. Sean Gaskie and Ms. Lin Max

GATX Corporation Matching Gifts

Ms. Irene Gawron

Mr. and Mrs. John W. Gay

Mrs. Elaine K. Geffen

Mr. and Mrs. Paul J. Geiger

Dr. Mary Gendernalik-Cooper and
    Mr. Wade Cooper

General Electric Foundation

Ms. Cynthia S. Gerber

Mr. and Mrs. William A. German

Mr. and Mrs. Andrew J. Gessow

Ms. Marie Gewirtz

Mr. and Mrs. Timothy Gieseke

Ms. Harriet A. Giles

Dr. Armand Gilinsky and
    Mrs. Josephine McCormick Gilinsky

Mr. and Mrs. Jerry Gill

Helga E. Gillies

Ms. Patricia J. Gingell

Ms. Vilma O. Ginzberg

Dr. Robert K. Girling and Ms. Sherry Keith

Mr. and Mrs. Donald Glickson

Global Impact

Mr. Robert W. Glover and Ms. Toni L. Falbo

Dr. and Mrs. James J. Glynn

Mrs. Margot Godolphin

Ms. Anne T. Goetsch

Ms. Helen L. Goldstein

Ms. Rachael M. Goldstein and
    Mr. Allen A. Ginsling

Mr. and Mrs. Judson E. Goodrich

Ms. Phyllis Goodwin

Ms. Denise Gordon

Ms. Lois K. Gordon

Mr. and Mrs. Michael Gough

Mr. and Mrs. D. John Graham

Mr. and Mrs. Richard P. Grahman

Ms. Natasha J. Granoff

Jule Adams Grant Fund

Mr. and Mrs. Richard J. Grant

Mr. James L. Grau

Mr. John S. Gravell

Audrey Gray

Mr. David S. Gray and Ms. Vrenae A. Sutphin

Ms. Mary Louise Greenberg

Ms. Martha J. Gregg

Ms. Dorothy Greninger

Ms. Joyce V. Griffin

Grill Concepts

Mr. and Mrs. Benjamin Gross

Dr. and Mrs. Tom Gross

Mr. and Mrs. Kevin Grubbs

Ms. Nora L. Guthrie

Ms. Joan D. Haigh

Mr. Charles Hall

Mr. and Mrs. Fred Hall

Mr. Douglas M. Hanchi

Dr. and Mrs. David F. Hanes

Ms. Marilyn Hannum

Mr. Herbert M. Hansen

Ms. Nancy Hansen

Ms. Natalie Hansen

Ms. Frances M. Harden

Mr. and Mrs. Gerald D. Hardy

J.V.K. and Fern Harger

Ms. Jean G. Hargrove

Mr. and Mrs. Mark A. Harmon

Mr. and Mrs. Jeff Harriman

Mr. Michael Harrington and
    Ms. Martha J. Frankel

Ms. Martha Hart and Mr. Henry Schulte

Mr. and Mrs. William Hart

Ms. Dorothy Haub

Mr. and Mrs. John Hawk

Ms. Marion Hawley

Mr. and Mrs. Will Haymaker

HDP Enterprises

Donald and Jane Head

Mr. and Mrs. Walter Heagy

Dr. and Mrs. Hyland Hebert

Sandy Heft

Mr. and Mrs. Donald Heid

Mr. and Mrs. Charles Helmick, Sr.

Mr. and Mrs. Andrew O. Hendrickson

Ms. Kristin A. Hermanson

Ms. Portia G. Herold

The Robert Hesse Charitable Fund

Mr. and Mrs. Michael J. Hickey

Mr. and Mrs. Clifford H. Higgerson

Mr. Norman L. Hill

Mr. and Mrs. Richard T. Hill

Ms. Carol J. Hintze

Ms. Millie Hirsch

Ms. Janice E. Hitchcock

Ms. Joanne Hockett

Mr. and Mrs. Robert Hoewing

Mr. and Mrs. Daniel Hoffenberg

Mr. and Mrs. Buzzy Hofheimer

Ms. Molly Hogan

Mr. and Mrs. Erik Holbek

Mrs. Polly Holbrook

Ms. Mary Holden

Mr. Robert B. Hope and Ms. Paula C. Hammett

Mr. Carlile Horn

Bob and Judi Howard

Mr. and Mrs. Jack L. Howard

Mr. and Mrs. William Howard

Mr. and Mrs. John C. Hudson

Dr. E. R. Hudspeth

Mr. and Mrs. Adam Huetter

Mr. and Mrs. Pete J. Hulsman

Mr. and Mrs. Cecil G. Humes

Mr. and Mrs. Thomas K. Hunt

Mrs. Ann Hunter

Ms. Lisa K. Hunter

Ms. Susan R. Hunter

Mr. and Mrs. Phil Hurst

Mr. and Mrs. Raymond Hurt

Ms. Marjorie M. Hutton

Hyman Enterprise

Ms. Joan Inman

Ms. Helen Issel

Ms. Ruth Iversen

J Vineyards and Winery

JAC Enterprises Inc.

Ms. Elaine L. Jacob

Mr. and Mrs. Donald A. Jacobs

Mr. and Mrs. Gordon Jacobs

Ms. Mary Lou Jacobsen

Ms. Bonnie Jeffreys

Ms. Vesta B. Jelte

Mr. and Mrs. Robert L. Jenkins

Mr. and Mrs. George Jewell

Jewish Community Foundation

John M. Bryan Family Fund

Johnson & Johnson

Ms. Ann F. Johnson

Mr. Bruce R. Johnson

Mr. and Mrs. Cedric Johnson

Ms. Jeanne C. Johnson

Mr. and Mrs. Jeffrey W. Johnson

Mr. and Mrs. Kenneth E. Jones

Mr. and Mrs. Robert Jones

Mr. Stephen K. Jones

Mr. Stefan Jonson and Ms. Rhoann Ponseti

Mr. and Mrs. Alan Kafton

Mr. and Mrs. Daniel Kahane

Ms. Hannelore S. Kahane

Ms. Lynda R. Kahane and Mr. Philip Welch

Mr. and Mrs. Eric Kahle

Ms. Lila Kane

Mr. and Mrs. Euijun Kang

Mr. and Mrs. John Kangas

Mr. and Mrs. Daniel E. Kaplan

Mr. and Mrs. David Karpilow

Mr. and Mrs. James Katon

Mr. and Mrs. Stuart E. Katz

Ms. Anne Kaufman

Dennis L. Keegan

Ms. Jeanne C. Kehoe

Mr. and Mrs. Joe Keith

Mr. and Mrs. John W. Keker

Kelisky Family Trust

Dr. and Mrs. Wayne Kellam

Ms. Alana C. Kelly

Mr. Weston B. Kendall

Kennfoods USA LLC

Mr. Charles Kent

Ms. Mary Kent

Ms. Kay Kerriden

Mr. Ronald Kertzner

Mr. and Mrs. David Kestenbaum

Mr. Peter F. Kilkus

Mr. and Mrs. Arnold King

Justice and Mrs. Donald B. King (Retired)

Ms. Beatrice J. Kinkead Blanchard

Ms. Yvonne J. Kirchenbauer

Ms. Fran Kirkwood

Ms. Irene Kivitz

Mr. William Klippert

Mr. and Mrs. Stephen Klum

Ms. Emily Knapp

Mr. and Mrs. Greg Knowlton

Mr. and Mrs. Lawrence Kocher

Mr. and Mrs. Richard H. Koehler

F. Korbel & Brothers

Dr. and Mrs. William Kortum, DVM

Mr. and Mrs. Alex Kraft

Mr. and Mrs. Robert W. Kramer

Mrs. Jean Kraus

Ms. Candace Krause

Mr. and Mrs. Melvyn Krauss

George Krevsky Gallery

Mr. and Mrs. Art Kruckman

Mr. and Mrs. Paul Kruger

Mr. Dennis Kuba and Ms. Rosanne Arthur

Mr. and Mrs. Mike Kuimelis

Ms. Sherrill Kuttner

La Gastronomica

Ms. Lillian Labes

Mr. and Mrs. Irwin M. Lachman

Mr. and Mrs. Byron Lai

Mr. and Mrs. Frank LaMarca

Dr. and Mrs. Kenneth C. Lamb

John V. Lammers

Ms. Bobbie Lamport

Mr. and Mrs. Keith Lampson

Landis Communications Inc.

Mr. Allan Lane and Mrs. Ann M. Montecuollo

Ms. Barbara Lane

Ms. Kathy A. Lane

Ms. Lucienne Lanson

Mr. and Mrs. Robert Larsen

Dr. and Mrs. Ralph E. Lassa II

Ms. Frances Lazear

Ms. Andrea Learned

Mrs. Gaye LeBaron

Dr. Ardath M. Lee

Ms. Debra N. Lehane

Dr. and Mrs. Raymond G. Lemieux

Mr. Raymond L. Lent

Ms. Susan Lentz

Mr. and Mrs. Stephan C. Leonoudakis

Mr. and Mrs. Dean Letcher

Mr. and Mrs. Eric J. Levy

Mr. and Mrs. Leandro Lewis

Mr. and Mrs. Leslie Lewis

Ms. Patricia S. Lewis

Mr. and Mrs. Richard Lewis

Mr. and Mrs. Marc Lewitter

Mr. and Mrs. Henry J. Libicki

Mr. and Mrs. Howard Lieben

Ms. Christina M. Lindh

Mr. and Mrs. Paul Lippman

Sid and Gerry Lipton

Mr. and Mrs. Guy Littman

Ms. Bonnie Lockett

Ms. Donna W. Long

Mr. Sidney E. Loomis

Ms. Marcia I. Lotter

Mr. and Mrs. Frederick J. Lourence

Mr. George Loveday

Ms. Irene Lucia

Ms. Dorothea R. Lyman

Mr. John Lynch

Ms. Kimberly Lynch

Mr. and Mrs. William Lynch

Ms. Linda S. Lyons

Mr. Melvin Lyons and Ms. Darlene Wilson

Ms. Nancy E. Lyons

MacDonald Dental Lab

Mr. Ken Macheras

Mr. and Mrs. Malcolm MacKinnon

Mr. John L. Macleod

Mr. and Mrs. Adrian J. MacNab

Jaci and James Maddern

Mag Trucking

Mr. Donald Magnin

Mr. and Mrs. Marvin Mahler

Mr. David Mahoney

Dr. and Mrs. Howard Maibach

Ms. Beth Maize

Ms. Berkeley A. F. Malm

Mr. Joseph Malmstrom

Ms. Rosemary Manchester

Mr. and Mrs. Larry Mandell

Ms. Prudence W. Manley

Mr. and Mrs. Alfred Mansoor

Jennifer Marano

Dr. and Mrs. Kenneth K. Marcus

Mr. Oliver Margolin

Mr. Ronald Marley and Ms. Kathleen Torgenson

Mr. Steve L. Marlowe and Ms. Joan E. Gates

Maxine Marmor

Ms. Kim Marois

Ms. Kay M. Marquet

Ms. Julie R. Marquette

Mrs. Jacqueline Marquis

Mr. and Mrs. Paul Marsh

Mr. and Mrs. Frank R. Marshall

Ms. Kathryn E. Marshall

Mr. and Mrs. Larry Marshall

Ms. Ginger Martin and Mr. Fred Favero

Ms. Miriam Martinson

Rev. and Mrs. William J. Marx

Dr. William H. Mason

Mr. and Mrs. Andrew H. Massie, Jr.

Mr. James Mavrogenis

Ms. Edna I. Maxwell

Mr. and Mrs. James A. McBride

Ms. Pauline McConnell

Mr. and Mrs. Charles B. McCormack

Ms. Dorothy S. McCray

Mr. and Mrs. Thomas McCrea

Ms. Phyllis McCreery

Ms. Thelma S. McCune

Ms. Marie J. McDermott

Mr. Nicholas McGegan

Mr. and Mrs. Richard McGoogan

Mr. Charles D. McGowan

Mr. and Mrs. Malcolm McIlroy

Mr. Carl W. McIntosh

Mr. and Mrs. Bob McIntyre

Mr. and Mrs. Paul McKairnes

Barbara M. McKee Trust

Ms. Velma McKelvey

Ms. Carolyn McKenna

Ms. Patricia McKowen

Ms. Ellen McNamara

Ms. Carol J. McNeil

Mr. and Mrs. Michael T. McQuillen

Mr. and Mrs. Douglas McVeigh

Mr. and Mrs. Phillip McWeeny

Mr. Kirke Mechem

Mr. and Mrs. William Meddaugh

Mr. Mark Meierding and Ms. Linda Lampson

Dr. Edith P. Mendez

Ms. Edith P. Menrath

Constance A. Menzies

Mr. and Mrs. Richard E. Merriss

Mr. Joseph E. Mesics

Mr. and Mrs. Bud L. Metzger

Ms. Eva Mikalson

Mr. Grant Miller

Dr. and Mrs. Jeffrey Miller

Mr. and Mrs. Jeffrey A. Miller

Mr. and Mrs. Marteen J. Miller

Ms. Sally M. Miller

Ms. Clare Millikan

Ms. Margaret C. Millner

Mr. and Mrs. Bruce Mitchell

Mr. and Mrs. Carl Mitchell

Mr. and Mrs. Jim Mogck

Dr. and Mrs. Glenn Molyneaux

Ms. Robbin Montero

Ms. Barbara M. Moore

Ms. Bonnie A. Moore

Ms. Laurie Moore

Ms. Patricia Moore

Ms. Melinda G. Moreaux

Mr. and Mrs. Donald S. Moritz

Mr. Michael Moritz and Ms. Harriet Heyman

Mr. and Mrs. James W. Morrison

Ms. Adele Mortensen

Ms. Marjorie Mortensen

Ms. Bonnie M. Morton

Mr. and Mrs. Paul Mowbray

Ms. Carol Muir

Mr. Richard D. Mulliner

Ms. Susan Mullins

Multi-Contact USA

Mr. and Mrs. Ned Mundell

Mr. Dennis Murphy and
    Mrs. Katie Wetzel Murphy

Ms. Mary L. Murphy and Mr. Claude Krummes

Ms. Sandra Murray

Mr. and Mrs. William B. Murray

Ms. Betsy Nachbaur

Michael and Shelley Nagel

Mr. and Mrs. Ronald Nakamoto

Mr. and Mrs. Clyde R. Nance

Ms. Janese Nank

National Association of Teachers

Ms. Janet Natov

Lawrence E. Nelson and Family

Ms. Karen Nelson-German

Ms. Karen Neureuter

New York Life Insurance

New York Times Foundation

Mr. Robby J. Nichol

Barbara S. Nichols

Mr. David S. Nichols

Mr. Robert L. Nichols and Ms. Patricia P. Givens

Ms. Eileen Nicholson

Dr. Mary Ann Nickel and Mr. Marv Nickel

Mr. and Mrs. William F. Niehous

Mrs. Virginia Noonan

Ms. Virginia Norman

NorthBay Nissan

Mr. and Mrs. Howard L. Norton

Norton Simon Museum of Art at Pasadena

Mr. and Mrs. Larry E. Nutting

Mr. and Mrs. Steven J. Oberle

Ms. Anthy O'Brien

Mr. and Mrs. Stephen D. O'Brien

Ms. Sara C. Obuchowski-Mitchell and
    Mr. Alex Mitchell

Dr. and Mrs. Eduardo Ochoa

O'Dell Printing Company

Mr. and Mrs. Mike O'Donnell

Mr. Ricky Okane

Genevieve O'Lague

Ms. Charlotte Oldaker

Mr. and Mrs. Ernest Olson

Ms. Lane E. Olson and Mr. Steven J. Stucky

Mrs. Maurine Olson

Margaret Olwell

Mr. and Mrs. Patrick O'Melveny

Mr. Patrick O'Melveny

Ms. Beverly Opelka

Dr. and Mrs. Rudolph O. Oppenheimer

Orion Medical Group

Mr. Mike Orton and Dr. Clarice Stasz

Dr. Stephen B. Oshry and
    Ms. Anne M. Lieberman

P.E.O. Sisterhood Chapter JO

Pacific Gas and Electric

Mr. and Mrs. John Palacios

Dr. and Mrs. Norman Panting

Dr. and Mrs. Roderic Park

Mr. and Mrs. William F. Park

Parke Industries

Mr. and Mrs. Keith Parker

Ms. Kim Parker

Ms. Joan Parsons

Mr. John S. Pashilk

Mrs. Laurie A. Patterson

Mrs. Charlotte P. Pedersen

Mr. and Mrs. Harold V. Pederson

Mr. and Mrs. Lee Peele

Elizabeth and Ralph Peer Fund

Ms. Stacey L. Pelinka

Mr. and Mrs. Michael L. Pendergast

Ralph and Patricia Pendleton

Mr. and Mrs. Sydney Perlman

Mr. and Mrs. Alec Peters

Ms. Joyce Peters

Mr. Ralph Peters

Ms. Tyffani Peters

Ms. Audrey N. Peterson

Bucky and Wendy Peterson

Mr. and Mrs. David Peterson

Mr. Robert M. Pew

Ms. Antreen Pfau

Pfizer Foundation Matching Gifts Program

PG&E Corporation Foundation

Mr. and Mrs. Edward Plant

Plastic Surgery Associates of
    Santa Rosa Medical Corp

Ms. Joan R. Platt

Dr. and Mrs. Gerhard Plaut

Mr. Lance M. Plaza

Ms. Ann M. Plubell

Ms. Betty L. Pommon

Ms. Carol Ponzio

Mr. and Ms. John R. Post

Mr. and Mrs. John W. Poulos

Mr. and Mrs. Frank Poulsen

Ms. Virginia Poust

Ms. Mary K. Praetzellis

James and Peggy Price

Mr. Fred F. Ptucha

Ms. Cheri K. Puig

Ms. Judith J. Purdom

Mr. and Mrs. Irving Rabin

Mr. and Mrs. Steve Rabinowitsh

Mr. and Mrs. Warren Radford

Mr. Karl Radtke and Ms. Diana Laczkowski

Ms. Kamilla Rajnus

Ms. Patricia E. Raley

Mr. and Mrs. Gary Ramatici

Mr. and Mrs. Walter Ramseur

Mr. and Mrs. Riley Rankin

Ms. Margaret S. Ray

Reader's Digest Foundation

Redwood Foundation

Ms. Jean M. Reed

Mr. and Mrs. Thomas Reed

Dr. Natalie Rees

Mr. Harold B. Reid and
    Mrs. Linda L. Loveland Reid

Ms. Joan Reid

Ms. Valerie J. Reid

Mrs. Carlene Reininga

Mr. and Mrs. Robert G. Reinking

Mr. and Ms. Larry Remington

Renesis Development

Mr. and Mrs. Clark Reynolds

Mrs. Kathleen A. Reynolds

Ms. Carolyn W. Rich

Mr. and Mrs. Charles Richard

Ms. Donna Richards

Mr. and Mrs. L. W. Richards

Ms. Camille Richardson

Mr. Michael Richardson

Mr. and Mrs. Sig Richardson

Mr. and Mrs. Pete Richmond

Ms. Roberta K. Rigney

Mrs. Mary Louise Riley

Mike and Sue Riley

Henry and Bernice Ring

Mr. and Mrs. Bob Ringo

John and Sue Riordan

Mr. Pete V. Rios

Ms. Jane O. Rising

RMG Capital Corporation

Mr. and Mrs. Barrett B. Roach

Mrs. LaPreal Robbins

Ms. Muriel L. Robbins

Mr. Keith L. Roberts

Dr. and Mrs. John Robinson

Mr. and Mrs. John M. Rock

Mr. and Mrs. Richard Rodkin

Rodney Strong Wine Estates

Mr. Larry Rogers and Ms. Julie Kimelman

Mr. and Mrs. Craig Roland

Mrs. Elayne Roland

Ms. Loria Rolander

Mr. William Ronchelli

Mr. and Mrs. Salvatore Rosano

Ms. Gaylene R. Rosaschi

Dr. and Mrs. K. Daniel Rose

Rose T. Rose

Mr. Wren Rose

Ron Rothert Insurance Services

Mr. and Mrs. David Rounds

Mr. Harry C. Rowe

RSF Innovations in Social Finance

Mr. and Mrs. Jack Rubin

Ms. Margaret J. Rued

Ms. Margret L. Ruehrdanz

Mr. and Mrs. Alfred F. Runner

Ms. Barbara C. Russell

Ms. Claire Russell

Mr. and Mrs. Robert D. Ryan

Mr. John Saari and Ms. Corinne Jones

Mr. Eugene Sabelman

Dr. and Mrs. Richard W. Sagebiel

Mr. and Mrs. Robert Sampson

Mr. and Mrs. Morgan Sanders

The Santa Rosa Dental Group

Santa Rosa Recycling and Collect

Ms. Lois B. Santero

Ms. Marlynn Sartori

Ms. Kris Saslow and Mr. George Sinclair

Mr. and Mrs. Julus M. Sassenrath

Ms. Yasuyo Satoh

Mr. and Mrs. David Saucer

Ms. Chai S. Savage

Mr. John N. Savage

Ms. Laura E. Sawyer

Mr. and Mrs. Samuel Scalise

Ms. Cynthia Scarborough

Mr. Albert Schadel

Mr. and Mrs. John Schiller

Ms. Kathie Schmid

Dr. and Mrs. Leon H. Schmidt

Mr. and Mrs. Henry A. Schmutz

David Schneider

Ms. June H. Schneider

Ms. Vreni Schnirman

Mr. and Mrs. Paul Schoch

Mr. Gene Schott and Ms. Joan M. Crowley

Mr. and Mrs. Alan F. Schroeder

Ms. Susan K. Schubring

Mr. and Mrs. James F. Schultz

Mr. and Mrs. Ralph Schultz

Ms. Ellen Schwab

Galen and Maxine Schwab

Ms. Sylvia Schwartz

Mr. Russell Schweickart and Ms. Nancy Ramsey

Ms. Rosalie Schweit

Mr. and Mrs. Mike Scofield

The Sea Ranch Construction Inc.

Mr. and Mrs. Robert Seastrom

Seattle Foundation

Mr. and Mrs. David A. Self

Mr. and Mrs. Jack H. Semple

Mr. and Mrs. Paul Sengstock

Mr. Richard Senn and Ms. Barbara Sachs

Mr. and Mrs. Michael D. Senneff

Robert Shapiro Family Foundation

Mr. and Mrs. Marvin Sharpe

Mr. and Mrs. Gary Shatto

Mr. Kurt Shaver

Ms. Perdita L. Sheirich

Mr. and Mrs. Adam Shelton

Mr. and Mrs. Marvin Sherak

Ms. Karen Shinozaki

Mrs. Arleen Shippey

Ms. Marlys Siegel

Mr. and Ms. Peter Siegenthaler

Mr. and Mrs. Don Siemens

Mr. and Mrs. Alan Silow

Mr. and Mrs. Mario Silvestri

Mr. Gerhard F. Simmel

Mr. Roger Simon

Mr. and Mrs. Calvin H. Simons

Mr. and Mrs. Lawrence Simons

Mr. and Mrs. Danny D. Simpson

Dr. and Mrs. Ronald G. Simpson

Mr. and Mrs. Duane Skogen

Mr. and Mrs. Louis J. Sloss, Jr.

Mr. and Mrs. Peter Slusser

Mr. and Mrs. Edward A. Small, Jr.

Mr. and Mrs. Joseph W. Small

Dr. Susan M. Smile

Ms. Michele D. Smirl

Mr. and Mrs. Steve Smit

Mr. Donald A. Smith

Dr. Fredrika P. Smith

Ms. Gloria M. Smith

Mr. and Mrs. Joseph Smith

Mr. Mikkel Smith

Mr. Timothy P. Smith

Mr. and Mrs. Gordon Smythe

Harold and Dorothy Soeters

Mr. Michael Sohigian

Ms. Jean Sokolinski

Sonoma Cardiology

Sonoma Co. Alumnae Panhellenic

Sonoma County Grape Growers

Sonoma County Tourism Bureau

Sonoma Valley Bancorp

Mr. and Mrs. Jerol M. Sonosky

Dr. and Mrs. Robert P. Sorani

Dr. and Mrs. L. R. Sorensen

Mr. Edward M. Sorenson and Mr. Ray Gallardo

Dr. and Mrs. Mitchell Soso

Ms. Marian Sotmary

Ms. Victoria M. Souder

Mr. and Mrs. James E. Spangler

Mr. and Mrs. Gary G. Specker

SpeeDee Oil

Mary and Walter Spellman Fund

Mr. and Mrs. G. S. Spence, Jr.

Mr. and Mrs. David Spilman

Mr. and Mrs. Morris Spizman

SSU Associated Students

Alice Staller

Mr. and Mrs. Howard Stanley

State Compensation Insurance Fund

Mr. and Mrs. Eric C. H. Steadman

Mr. and Mrs. John Steadman

Mr. Preston S. Stedman

Ms. Kat Stephens

Mr. and Mrs. Gary Stetzel

Ms. Lisa Stevens

Mr. Richard W. Stevens and
    Ms. Virginia L. Behm

Mr. Hugh C. Stevenson and Ms. Diane L.
    Paleczny-Stevenson

Mr. and Mrs. Benjamin R. Stewart

Mr. and Mrs. Richard Still

Dr. and Mrs. Daniel P. Stites

Ms. Marilyn Stockfleth

Ms. Marilyn J. Stocks

Mr. and Mrs. Howard S. Stoddard

Steve Stolen and Rob MacPherson

Mr. Ben Stone

Ms. Hannah Stone

Mr. and Mrs. John Strickley

Sugarloaf Farming Corporation dba
    Peter Michael Winery

Sullivan Birney Ranch

Summers-McCann

Sunday Symposium of Oakmont

Ambassador and Mrs. Louis Susman

Mr. and Mrs. Stephen G. Sussman

Rosemary Suttie

Mr. and Mrs. Thomas S. Swan, Jr.

Mr. and Mrs. John S. Swift, Jr.

Mr. Marshall Taxer and Ms. Debra Crow

Team North Construction Services, Inc.

Mr. and Mrs. John C. Temple-Raston

Dr. and Mrs. Joseph S. Tenn

Mr. James Tetrud and Ms. Karen L. Butterfield

Dr. Elizabeth and Mr. Mike Thach

Mr. and Ms. David S. Theis

Dr. Hobart F. Thomas

Ms. Sally Thomas

Dr. Sue A. Thomas

Mr. and Mrs. Britton R. Thompson

Thompson Insurance Agency, Inc.

Ms. Mary Thompson

Mr. and Mrs. Don Thoreson

Mr. Roy D. Thylin and
    Ms. Brunhilde W. Simmons

Mrs. Kathy L. Tidwell

Mr. and Ms. H. T. Tiemens

Dr. Paul Tiernan

Mr. and Mrs. Otis G. Tippit

Mr. and Mrs. Thomas Tomasi

Ms. Barbara Tomin

Ms. Millicent Tomkins

Top Speed Data Communications

Ms. Ann-Marie Totman

Mr. and Mrs. Donald H. Trahan

Ms. Lynda Trombetta Angell

Mr. and Ms. R. Scott Trumbull

Paul Tuell

Mr. and Mrs. James Tunzi

Mr. Jeffrey B. Turnbull

Mr. Alexander J. Turner

Ms. Marilyn S. Turner

Mrs. Roberta Turner

Ms. Mary G. Tuscher

Mr. and Mrs. Jim Tutt

Ms. Jean P. Tyacke

Mr. and Mrs. Toby Tyler

Ms. Elizabeth Tynan

Ms. Krista Uhl

Union Bank of California

Union Bank of California Foundation

United Way California Capital Region

Del and Olive Valleau

Capt. and Mrs. Gerald Van Norden (Retired)

Ms. Ann Vander Ende

Ms. Dorothy Vandergoot

Mr. Carl Verduin

Mr. and Mrs. Todd Verke

Mr. and Mrs. Charles A. Vetrano

Mr. and Mrs. Antonio Vicini

Mr. and Mrs. James A. Vick

Mr. and Mrs. Frank J. Vineyard

Vinquiry

Dr. and Mrs. Michael Visser

Viva Foundation

Mr. and Mrs. Joe Vivio

Ms. Jan L. Volk

Mr. and Mrs. Arthur J. Volkerts

Mr. John Volz and Ms. M. S. Patton-Volz

Ms. Alice Waco

Jane Wagner

Ms. Julia Wakelee-Lynch

Mr. and Mrs. Harold Walba

Elena Madison Walker Charitable Trust

Ms. Rosemary J. Waller

Ms. Virginie H. Walsh

Mr. Jeffrey A. Walter and
    Mrs. Valerie Pistole-Walter

Mr. and Mrs. Dennis Warren

Mr. Tim Warren and Ms. Sabrina Braham

Ms. Ellen Watson and Ms. Elisabeth Watson

Mr. David Wattell

Ms. Moira Watts

Dr. and Mrs. Charles K. Wear

Mr. and Mrs. Charles R. Webb

Mr. Edward Weber

Ms. Karen Wedsted

Mr. and Mrs. Jack L. Weeks

Ms. Patricia L. Wegman

Ms. Cynthia L. Weichel

Mr. and Mrs. Robert G. Weil

Mr. and Mrs. George Weiner

Ms. Ann Weinstock

Mr. and Mrs. Gerald Weissman

Mr. and Mrs. Barton Weitzenberg

Mr. Arthur Welch

Mr. David Welch

Mrs. Sally Welch

Ms. Georgia E. Welles

Ms. Carmen G. Welling

Wells Fargo Educational Foundation

Mr. and Mrs. Kenneth G. Wells

Ms. Ruth E. Wells

Mr. Jason E. Wenrick

Mr. and Mrs. Jay Werth

Mr. and Mrs. Richard West

Mr. and Mrs. Richard P. West

Mr. and Ms. Philip Westergaard

Mr. and Mrs. G. C. Wheeler

Mr. and Mrs. Donald F. Whistler, Jr.

Mr. and Mrs. David Whorton

Florence Wickham

Ms. Mary Jane Wickham

Ms. Tami Wiener-Stout

Ms. Carolyn A. Wiester

Dr. Sharon Wiles

Mr. and Mrs. Neil W. Wiley

Ms. Wendy P. Wiley

Mr. and Mrs. Randall Willens

Mr. and Mrs. Charles Williams

Ms. Rose A. Williams

Ms. Elizabeth W. Williamson

Mr. Paul W. Willihnganz and
    Ms. Geraldine A. French

Dr. Janice L. Wilson

Winery Exchange

Mr. and Mrs. Edward M. Winfield

Ms. Sandra Wiseley

Ruth and David Wolf

Ms. Jean Wollan

Ms. Mary F. Wood

Ms. Suzanne Wood

The Honorable Lynn C. Woolsey

World Reach

Gordon Wright

Mr. and Mrs. Gerold Wunderlich

Mr. and Mrs. James J. Wycoff

Ms. Sarah Yardley

Ms. Jean M. Young

Young's Market Company

Mr. Paul Zamarian and Ms. Sandy Jay

Mr. Bob Ziegler

Mr. and Mrs. Gene Zierdt

Ms. Thea Zimmerman

Ms. Joy L. Zindell

Mr. and Mrs. Samuel Zucker

Mr. and Mrs. Gene E. Zundel

Photo Credits

Index